canoeing

canoeing

JOHN MALO

FOLLETT PUBLISHING COMPANY • CHICAGO • NEW YORK

The author wishes to thank the Foreman High School students and the University of Miami students who appear in many of the photographs in this book. He also gratefully acknowledges the following for permitting the reproduction of photographs on the indicated pages:

JOSEPH K. BENGTSON, *page 126*
BLACK STAR, TED ROZUMALSKI, *front cover;* FRED KAPLAN, *page 37*
CANADIAN CENTENNIAL COMMISSION 1967, *pages 124 and 125*
CANADIAN GOVERNMENT TRAVEL BUREAU, *page 112*
GRUMMAN BOAT COMPANY, *pages 49 and 91*
JIM KRZEMINSKI, *pages 24, 38, 41, 42, 43, 46, 57, 58, 65, 73, and 75*
JOE MIGON, *pages 51, 60, 62, 64, 66, and 71*
MINNESOTA DEPARTMENT OF ECONOMIC DEVELOPMENT, *pages 85 and 99*
MINNESOTA HISTORICAL SOCIETY, *original painting by Mrs. Frances E. Hopkins, page 120*
OLD TOWN CANOE COMPANY, *pages 19, 35, and 67*
PUBLIC ARCHIVES OF CANADA, *original painting by Mrs. Frances E. Hopkins, page 119*
CLYDE H. SMITH, *pages 2, 3, 10, 25, 78, and 123*
PHILIP E. VIERLING, *page 21*

The line drawings on pages 13, 31, 40, 52, and 109 are by RAY NAYLOR.

SBN 695-41035-0   Titan binding
SBN 695-81035-9   Trade binding

Library of Congress Catalog Card Number: 69-10252

First Printing
D

CONTENTS

INTRODUCTION

As coach of the United States Olympic Canoeing Team, I work with expert canoeists, who represent the top of American performers. Before a canoeist reaches Olympic status, he has a wealth of instructions to absorb, a great number of hours to train, and a valuable experience to live.

Olympic participation is not for the average canoeist—just as ski jumping is not for the weekend skier, nor Mount Everest for the amateur mountain climber. However, basic canoeing skills can be learned by almost anyone, regardless of age, and can lead to unforgettable adventure. Reading this book, which gives elementary lessons in the sport of canoeing, is the way to begin.

The training for athletic competition on a high level is

rigorous and demanding, yet canoeists are so close to nature that they enjoy it. The physical development of the body is tremendous, and the atmosphere of racing is exciting. The thrill of canoeing competition, and coaching people of all walks of life, gives me the greatest personal satisfaction. I feel sure you will find the sport of canoeing equally rewarding.

GERT R. GRIGOLEIT

COACH, UNITED STATES
OLYMPIC CANOEING TEAM

Gert R. Grigoleit, Coach of the United States Olympic Canoeing Team, leaves for competition at the 1964 Olympics, in Tokyo, Japan.

8

ABOUT GERT R. GRIGOLEIT

Holder of canoeing and kayaking championships in two countries, Gert R. Grigoleit began learning watercraft skills as a boy in Königsberg, Germany. As a member of a kayak club, he entered many local and regional races and won numerous prizes.

Eventually his mastery of the sport led him into national competition in kayaking. He participated in single, two-man, and four-man events. He and his teammates captured the German national championship in the 1952 four-man kayak race, and in 1954 he and his partner won the two-man race.

Shortly after this, Mr. Grigoleit immigrated to the United States. He became a naturalized American citizen in 1962.

To his new country, Mr. Grigoleit brought his talent and enthusiasm for canoeing and kayaking. He became the North American kayaking champion in 1961 and in 1963. Then he qualified for the 1964 United States Olympic Canoeing Team. After his performance at the Games in Tokyo, Japan, he was named Coach of the United States Canoeing Team, which competed under his direction in the 1968 Olympics in Mexico City, Mexico.

Mr. Grigoleit holds an engineering degree from a university in Munich, Germany. He is married and lives in Sacramento, California, where he owns a construction business. When not working or canoeing, he pursues his other sports interests, participating in sailing, skiing, and cycling competition.

9

CHAPTER ONE

KNOW YOUR CANOE

Throughout the ages, certain words and phrases have been used to describe parts of ships both large and small. From captain to cabin boy, each officer and crew member had to know his ship thoroughly so that he could carry out orders.

Knowing the exact names of the parts of your craft is equally important in the sport of canoeing. When you are acquainted with the parts of your canoe, you will be able to respond promptly to an instructor's commands. As a member of a paddling team, or with a group in a canoe, you will use the same terms as your fellow canoeists and so will work with them more smoothly. You will also be able to discuss the sport intelligently with other canoe enthusiasts.

To learn the various parts of a canoe and their positions, study the diagram of a typical canoe. As you can see, the front of the canoe is called the bow. Accordingly, such parts as bow seat, bow deck, and bow thwart are located in the forward section. The

Knowledge of their craft and of canoeing skills enables these two paddlers to cruise the swiftly moving White River in Vermont.

stern is the rear of the canoe, and it identifies the location of such parts as stern seat, stern deck, and stern line.

The following list will help you to identify the parts and to understand certain terms commonly used in boating.

CANOE TERMS

Ahead: Ahead of the canoe.
Amidships: The middle section of the canoe.
Astern: Behind the canoe.
Bang plate: See *Stemband*.
Beam: Width of the canoe at its widest part.
Bow: The forward end of the canoe.
Bowman: The person who paddles from the front, or bow, seat.
Deck: The flat, triangular-shaped watertight piece of wood on the top of the bow and stern ends, to which the gunwales converge and attach. Also called *wedge*.
Draft: The depth of water that a canoe draws or displaces.
Freeboard: The distance from the waterline to the gunwale.
Gunwale: The upper edge of the side of a canoe; pronounced *gunnel*.
Hull: The hollow, lowermost portion of a canoe.
Inwale: A strip of wood placed inside the planking at the sheer line, and a part of the gunwale assembly.

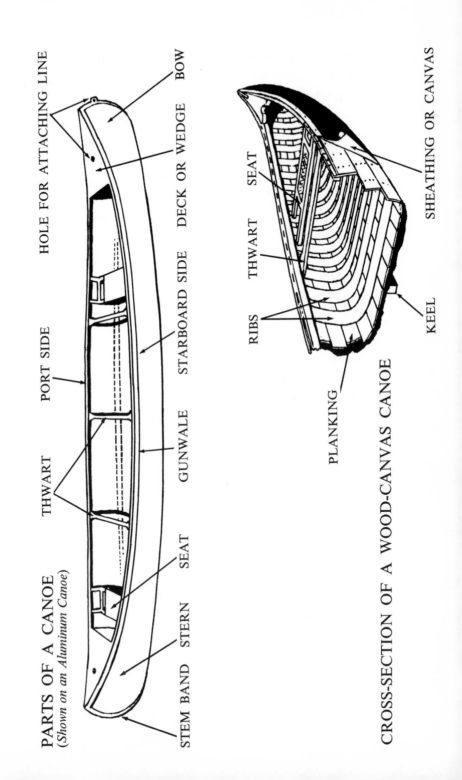

PARTS OF A CANOE
(Shown on an Aluminum Canoe)

HOLE FOR ATTACHING LINE

BOW

DECK OR WEDGE

PORT SIDE

STARBOARD SIDE

THWART

GUNWALE

SEAT

STEM BAND   STERN

CROSS-SECTION OF A WOOD-CANVAS CANOE

SHEATHING OR CANVAS

SEAT

THWART

RIBS

KEEL

PLANKING

Keel: A strip of wood or metal on the outside of the canoe that runs along the center of the bottom from the bow to the stern.

Leeward: The direction toward which the wind is blowing.

Line: The rope, sometimes called a *painter*, used to tie up or tow a canoe.

Outwale: The portion of the gunwale assembly that is attached to the outside of the planking.

Planking: The thin cedar boards that cover the outside of the ribs of a wood-canvas canoe, and give a smooth surface on which the canvas is applied.

Port: The left side of the canoe as you sit or kneel facing the bow.

Ribs: On wood-canvas canoes, strong curved strips of wood that extend down the sides and across the bottom from gunwale to gunwale.

Sheathing: See *Planking*.

Sheer: The upward curve of the bow and stern as seen from the sides.

Starboard: The right side of the canoe as you sit or kneel facing the bow.

Stemband: A metal strip attached to the curved ends of the bow and stern of the canoe to protect these delicate edges from damage.

Stern: The back, or rear, of the canoe.

Sternman: The person who paddles from the rear, or stern, seat.

Thwart: A brace or crossbar extending across the top of the canoe from gunwale to gunwale; usually three in number; also called a *spreader*.

Windward: The direction from which the wind is blowing.

Yaw: To sway unintentionally from the intended course.

Although the terms listed are the accepted ones in the sport, canoemen in certain regions of the country may use a local lingo. These terms or their pronunciation may have been handed down through generations of people in the community. Don't dispute their use or argue that your term is correct. Just be sure you know what is meant by each word. A polite question usually prompts a generous explanation. Use the local terms with the local people.

TYPES OF CANOES   Twenty years ago approximately six companies made canoes. Today there are over 65 canoe manufacturers. They produce many types of canoes that differ in size, shape, and construction material. Although various canoes have their distinct advantages, the size and type are first considerations.

The most popular canoes range in length from 12 to 18 feet and, depending on their material, weigh from 50 to 110 pounds. To get the most out of the sport, the beginner should try a middle-sized canoe measuring 16 or 17 feet. Canoes of this size have many advantages: ease of transporting, ideal for two paddlers, and a capability of safely carrying three people and duffel up to 600 pounds.

Canoes less than 12 feet long, though fine for solo paddling, have less carrying capacity, and their use on large lakes and fast rivers is limited. Canoes larger than 17 feet are work canoes, used primarily by professional woodsmen who freight heavy cargoes. They are also used for recreational canoeing in camp programs and on extended canoe-camping trips. In these situations, the disadvantage of their heavy weight is offset by their usefulness in carrying many passengers and up to a ton of cargo.

The weight of a canoe of a certain length varies with the construction materials used. Eighteen-foot models made of wood and canvas weigh approximately 90 pounds. Aluminum canoes of that length weigh about 85 pounds, and fiber glass models are about 75 pounds. To determine the approximate weight of a canoe, add eight pounds for each foot over 18 feet, and deduct eight pounds for each foot under 18 feet.

Like weight, canoe prices vary with the materials used. On the average, an 18-foot canoe would range in price from $265 for fiber glass to $275 for aluminum and $320 for wood-canvas. You may use this simple rule to find the approximate cost of other sized canoes. Add $15 for each foot of length over 18 feet; deduct $15 for each foot shorter than 18 feet. Prices are subject to change and vary widely among canoe manufacturers. If you buy directly from a manufacturer, you will have to pay shipping and freight charges.

You needn't worry about the design of canoes produced by reputable companies. Such firms as Chestnut Canoe Co. Ltd., Fredericton, New Brunswick, Canada; Old Town Canoe Company, Old Town, Maine; Grumman Boats, Marathon, New York; Aluma Craft Boat Division, Alpex Corporation, Minneapolis, Minnesota; and other progressive and competitive manufacturers have spent great sums of money on research to produce quality crafts. Their canoes are well engineered, carefully constructed, and material tested for efficient and safe handling. In general, their middle-sized models feature a flat straight bottom, a shallow keel, and a long waterline. These features give the craft stability, allow it to skim over the water with easy paddling, and enable it to hold its course with little guidance.

Modern manufacturers use a wide variety of materials in their canoes—wood-canvas, plywood, aluminum, and fiber glass. Each type of craft offers different qualities to the canoeist, who must select the kind best suited to his needs. The beginner should study all available literature about the various canoes and compare it critically before making his purchase.

THE WOOD-CANVAS CANOE   In principle —that is, in shape and design—the wood-canvas canoe of today is similar to the Indians' original birchbark canoe.

For their craft, the Indians cut cedar ribs and

then steamed and formed them into curves. A thin sheathing of black spruce was placed over the ribs the length of the form. Then the crosspieces, or thwarts, were anchored to the gunwales to give the craft its structural shape. The birchbark was applied to the outside of the sheathing, then glued at the seams with spruce gum. At the two ends and over the gunwales, the birchbark was sewn with resilient spruce roots or rawhide.

The finished creation was a lightweight, sturdy craft, capable at once of freighting heavy loads and of moving rapidly. Its silent-cruising feature made it ideal for stalking animals, birds, and enemies.

Toward the end of the 19th century, because of the shortage of bark in some areas, the birchbark gave way to the wood-canvas canoe of white-man construction. Throughout the years, this canoe has been improved in many ways.

The ribs of wood-canvas canoes are made of white cedar, the toughest lightweight wood obtainable. Straight-grained red cedar is used as planking to cover the outside of the ribs, because of its excellent characteristic of splitting cleanly and readily when dry and seasoned. Mahogany, with its hard, durable quality, is used for the gunwales. Only rustproof galvanized nails and brass screws and hardware are used in the construction.

Once the canoe is formed, the wood is sanded smooth, and natural varnish is applied. A sheet of canvas is centered on the upturned canoe, pulled tight with canvas-stretching tackle, and nailed down from amidships toward the curve of the stems. Surplus canvas is trimmed off. Then the gunwales, keel, and stembands are screwed in place. White lead or plastic base filler is applied to the canvas in preparation for the high gloss waterproof paint. A variety of colors is available, making the finished craft bright and beautiful as well as highly resistant to damage.

Many veteran canoeists favor the wood-canvas canoe. They claim that such creations, each hand-crafted, make available a much greater selection of types and lengths. In addition, they like the quiet operation of the wood-canvas canoe.

The foundation for this wood-canvas canoe is a cedar frame, which will be covered with canvas and fitted with a floor rack and seats.

The wood-canvas canoe has two disadvantages, however. First, it tends to increase in weight. On an extended canoe trip, it can absorb as much as 15 pounds of water. A new paint job in spring can add another 10. Second, it requires rather extensive regular care—systematic winter storage, painting, varnishing, and recanvasing.

Despite these disadvantages, though, many canoeists find a certain appeal in a canoe fashioned by skilled craftsmen and resembling most closely the beautiful birchbark craft of the American Indian.

THE ALUMINUM CANOE   Just as the wood-canvas canoe succeeded the Indian birchbark, the aluminum canoe seems to be replacing the wood-canvas craft. It appears to have captured the fancy of the present generation of canoeists and campers. The overwhelming public demand for the metal craft probably comes from a desire to take advantage of new materials and the ingenuity of nautical engineers. By adapting the forming and riveting techniques used in naval and amphibious aircraft construction, manufacturers have made the aluminum canoe lightweight, sturdy, and durable.

The basis of the aluminum canoe is a tough hull construction. As in building aluminum aircraft, all curved surfaces of the canoe are cold-formed on stretch presses. A sheet of aluminum is stretched over a forming die, and a press, capable of exerting extreme pressure, shapes the rectangular sheet into a curved form that becomes one-half of the canoe. After being trimmed, drilled, and heat-treated, the two halves are riveted together. Then the gunwales, thwarts, seats, and decks are added. After careful assembly, the canoe is water-tested in huge tanks to assure a leak-proof hull. Most aluminum canoes are guaranteed for the lifetime of the original purchaser.

The aluminum canoe boasts many fine features. It incorporates all the desirable design elements of its ancestors—pointed ends, graceful lines and proportions, and a much flatter bottom than is possible with wood construction. An increased load capacity and greater stability are also features. Because of its

The aluminum canoe is lightweight but extremely rugged and damage resistant.

shallow draft, or ability to float in little water, it provides great maneuverability. The elimination of bowed ends gives it a longer waterline, which prevents the canoe from swaying or yawing.

The aluminum canoe is virtually impossible to sink. Plastic foam or air chambers, built in at the ends, increase the canoe's buoyancy. When upset, the craft usually rights itself, so paddlers can climb back aboard. Even when filled with water, the canoe will support more persons clinging to the gunwales than it would normally carry inside when floating upright.

In cruising situations, the standard aluminum canoe, with its rugged hull construction, slides past sandbars and over rocks, logs, and other obstructions. It resists punctures and tears better than any other type of canoe. And should it become dented, the bulges can be pounded out in the same way as an automobile fender.

In addition, the aluminum canoe does not warp or become waterlogged, is relatively free from care, and can be stored outside during all seasons. When used in fresh water, it does not require paint to protect the surface, although paint may be desired to reduce glare.

Practical as it is, however, the aluminum canoe is not without disadvantages. During extensive summer use, it absorbs heat from the sun and becomes hot to the touch. In cold weather, the chill of the metal can be transferred to your feet and knees. To some canoeists, other shortcomings of the aluminum canoe are the metallic sound of waves against its sides and the harsh, cold look of its metal body. They claim that a canoe of stamped, riveted, and welded material that sounds tinny and reflects sun glare is not pleasant to hear, see, or touch.

The thousands of happy owners of aluminum canoes shrug off these criticisms. They consider them to be minor, and claim that the metal craft's many excellent features outweigh its shortcomings. They point out that Canadian Indians and trappers, whose lives revolve around the use of a canoe, are now buying aluminum canoes.

THE FIBER GLASS CANOE   A newcomer in the field is the fiber glass canoe, made of woven glass fibers. To construct it, two layers of woven glass cloth and one layer of glass mat are molded into shape. They are bonded together with a resin adhesive to which color has been added for a permanent paint job. Sleek color choices and combinations are available.

The process of fiber glass construction varies widely among the various manufacturers. Each claims that its product is "as tough as steel." Although this is an exaggeration, the use of woven glass fiber reenforcement makes the canoe almost impossible to puncture.

Molded fiber glass construction offers canoeists many benefits. It eliminates the need for ribs and

The lack of thwarts and ribs on a molded fiber glass canoe provides extra space for passengers and cargo.

provides a smooth flat floor not found in other canoes. The use of thwarts for cross bracing is often unnecessary, leaving more open space for cargo and passengers. The material is also sufficiently pliable to permit the canoe bottom to flex in tight quarters, thus closely approximating the handling qualities of the original birchbark and wood-canvas canoes.

To guarantee more strength, greater stability, and adequate flotation, the fiber glass canoe is heavily laminated on the bottom. Check the foam-type flotation units to make certain they are placed in the bow and the stern, not under the seats.

Heavy weight and high cost are the drawbacks to fiber glass canoes. Engineers in the near future will probably resolve these disadvantages and produce a competitor to the other kinds of canoes. Some manufacturers predict that eventually a lightweight and incredibly strong fiber glass craft will exceed the aluminum canoe's advantages.

SPECIALIZED CANOES   Some of these materials are used in specialized canoes designed for purposes other than general cruising. Such canoes range from the 8-foot model for solo paddling on calm waters to the 34-foot freighter or war canoe for carrying huge loads and many passengers on large bodies of water.

A solo canoeist, equipped with safety helmet and double-bladed paddle, maneuvers his racing canoe through the rapids.

Freighter canoes provide pleasure and transportation for large groups. This model is constructed of fiber glass that simulates birchbark.

The modern freight canoes are built of heavy planking and ribbing covered with canvas or with fiber glass that is colored to simulate the original birchbark. This canoe, which can carry a crew of 15, is used for freighting goods, for recreation, and in pageants depicting historical events.

The racing canoe, built for speed, features a narrow beam and a low silhouette with a rounded bottom. Because of its light weight, the all-cedar canoe is ideal as a racing craft.

CANOE KITS   The basic principles of canoe design were difficult for the original Indian craftsmen to embody in a fine craft. Building a quality canoe was no easier for the ingenious explorers who followed. Therefore, it is not surprising that most modern "do-it-yourself" fans will be unable to achieve adequate standards of beauty, style, and safety in a homemade canoe.

26

Panel-plywood and fabric-over-framework canoe kits, usually under $50, are offered. They require a highly skilled craftsman to make them approximate in appearance the pictures of the finished model. Most magazine-design models are questionable in balance, seaworthiness, and dependability. Because homemade canoes may become dangerous cloth-covered frames, they are not recommended.

BUYING A USED CANOE   A good alternative to a new canoe is a well-maintained used canoe. These are generally considerably less expensive than brand-new models.

When considering a second-hand canoe, you must check it much more thoroughly and carefully than is necessary with a new canoe. Use the following list as an examination checklist.

1. Carefully examine the planking for rot, and check for cracked ribs that spring outward and bulge the canvas.

2. Look for deterioration of fabric covering, especially along the gunwales, along the keel, and around both decks.

3. Check for peeling paint and try to determine the number of coats applied during the life of the craft.

4. Keep away from canoes with round bottoms, narrow beams, and short hulls.

5. Look for canoes made by reputable firms. Never consider a used homemade canoe.

6. Check fiber glass canoes and molded canoes for hairline cracks or breaks that alter the lines of the hull.

7. Check the inner stems and the keel line of aluminum canoes for loose rivets; check the thwarts and seats for loose bolts.

8. Check screws and nails for rust unless brass ones were used.

9. Invert the canoe and sight down its length to see if the hull is sprung and out of shape.

10. If the structural skeleton of a canoe is sound and only the outer covering is defective, you may want to strip off the fabric to the bare wood and re-cover with canvas or fiber glass. On the used aluminum canoe, an added bolt and nut can be used to repair a loose thwart or seat, and rivets can be pounded to close up a deck, a loose keel strip, or other leaky seams.

RENTING A CANOE   If you cannot buy any kind of canoe, you can still enjoy canoeing, for canoe rental agencies are now found in most parts of the country. These agencies make it unnecessary for a beginner to own a canoe, paddles, or accessories.

Most agencies are located near canoeing waters —lakes, park ponds, water impoundments, or portions of rivers—where a canoe is rented, used locally, and returned to the rental dock. In general, the charge for canoe rental varies from $3 to $5 a day, with cheaper rates on weekdays.

Operators on a river-front location usually offer a pick-up service to bring canoes and passengers back to the launching site after a trip. This service eliminates the need for paddling upstream and back-tracking a route.

The charge for picking up a canoe party varies with the length of the trip. A pick-up from a 10-mile canoe float is approximately $2; a 30-mile float usually costs $4 for the party. The operators use cars with cartop carriers for single canoe pick-ups, and small trailers with canoe racks for large parties, such as church groups and Scout troops having or renting several canoes.

The greatest concentration of canoe rental agencies, or outfitters, is on the highly popular canoeing waters of Minnesota, Michigan, Wisconsin, Pennsylvania, New York, Maine, and Canada. There vacationists of all ages combine canoeing and

For group trips, a special trailer with built-in racks carries six canoes.

camping in beautiful wilderness settings.

However, all canoe rental agencies are not close to waterways. Some of the most popular are located in cities, far from the water's edge. Their available equipment includes such items as cartop carriers, tie cords, paddles, backrests, and crew seats, which may be rented for any period of time from one day to several weeks. Many of their customers are vacationing families bound for some favorite lake or stream.

The modern canoe rental enterprise has grown into an imaginative business in the past few years. A most versatile agency is the Chicagoland Canoe Base, offering sales and rentals of over 50 models ranging from an 8-foot canoe for solo paddling to a 34-foot voyageur canoe for 18 passengers. The firm's fiber glass copies of the original birchbark canoes of the fur traders are in great demand for pageants and historical reenactments of early explorers.

CANOE CARE   Because of their light weight, canoes are not so difficult to store as heavier boats. The important thing is to keep them off the ground so that the bottom of the hull is not damaged.

The ideal storage place is indoors—in a garage, basement, or barn. With a pulley arrangement from the rafters, the canoe can be hoisted up so that it does not occupy floor space. To hoist the canoe, use two rope loops or slings that fit under the bow and stern ends.

If it is necessary to store a canoe outdoors when not in use, an adequate rack can be made of two sawhorses. Set up the sawhorses so that about one-fourth of the canoe's length extends beyond each horse. Place the canoe upside down across the two sawhorses. Chain and padlock it to the horses to discourage theft.

For better support during storage, you can build a simple rack to keep the canoe off the ground. First, anchor firmly in the ground two upright fence posts. As with the sawhorses, place the posts far enough apart so that one-fourth of the canoe's length extends beyond each post. To each post, nail a 2″ x 4″ crosspiece that is a little longer than the width of the canoe; the two T-shaped crosspieces should face each other. Invert the canoe, rest it on the cross-pieces, and lash it to them. Chain and padlock the canoe to the rack.

T-RACK FOR CANOE STORAGE

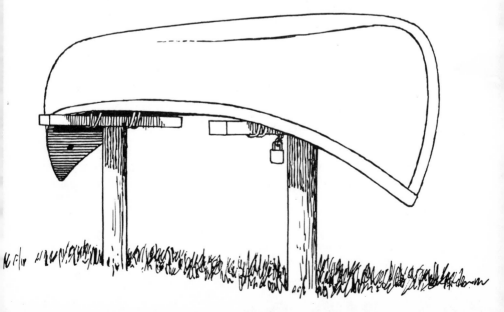

At a picnic or campsite, the canoe can be carried up on shore for brief periods. For longer periods, as in overnight camping, the canoe should be carried far from the water's edge and turned upside down for storage.

Whenever you go canoeing, you should carry an emergency repair kit. This will help you to avoid the unpleasant situation of being delayed or stranded because of minor damage to your canoe.

The kit should contain materials suitable for mending the canoe you are paddling. For the wood-canvas canoe, include muslin or canvas, ambroid cement, epoxy cement, or other quick-drying waterproof adhesive. Take cold aluminum compound in a tube for the aluminum canoe. Polyester fiber glass mat patch and quick-drying bond are necessary for the fiber glass craft, and can also be used on the wood-canvas canoe. These materials can be purchased at most boat, automotive, and hardware supply stores. In each case, follow exactly the instructions given on the items.

Besides patching materials, your repair kit should include a pair of scissors, a small hammer, and carpet tacks. All items should be stored in a waterproof bag and stowed in a packsack or the prow of the canoe.

With the modern materials available for patching aluminum and fiber glass canoes, the biggest repair problem is posed by wood-canvas canoes. Therefore, simple mending procedures are outlined below.

Generally, canvas rips in a long straight line or an L-shaped tear. Cut the patching cloth, rounding the corners, so that it overlaps the tear by an inch on all sides. Remove all sand and mud from the repair area; then dry the planking and canvas thoroughly. Apply a thin coat of adhesive to the wood and under the frayed fabric, and press it down. Next, apply a thin coat of cement to both the underside of the patch and the area on the canoe that it is to cover. Place the patch in position. Rolling a can over the repair works well in smoothing the patch over the break.

For a better patch, two layers of repair cloth should be used. The first patch is worked under the original canvas with a knife blade and is glued to the bare, clean, dry planking. Then the torn canvas is pulled together and pressed tightly over the first patch. The outside patch, overlapping the torn area, is added as described above. When the adhesive is dry, matching paint color is applied, followed by a few coats of spar varnish.

Where planking or ribs are cracked, they should be pressed into their original shape, splinted if necessary, and glued into place before the canvas patch is applied.

If you are caught without the recommended repair materials, you can temporarily mend a hole with waterproof adhesive tape, chewing gum, or the sticky pitch from spruce or balsam trees mixed with bacon grease. These patches must be replaced by more dependable and permanent repairs when you make camp for the night or return home.

All canoes have a long life if properly handled and cared for. Don't push or pull your canoe on land the way some campers handle rowboats, and don't use the upturned canoe as a sitting bench. After each trip, examine the canoe's underside and touch up with glue any developing weak spots or punctures. Also, drain accumulated water, and wipe all sand, twigs, and mud out of the canoe's interior with a sponge or rag. During the cold season, store it off the ground, out of the sun, and protect against strong winds. Treated in this way, your canoe will bring you many years of sporting fun.

CANOE VARIATIONS   Canoe sailing is a specialized form of the sport of canoeing. You can own an inexpensive sailboat by equipping your canoe with a simple sail and a few accessories.

Convert your canoe to a sailing craft with a sailing unit manufactured specifically for canoes. The unit fits any standard model canoe, and eliminates the complicated installation tasks of drilling holes and attaching the mast, spars, rigging, leeboards, and rudder. The aluminum accessories are engineered so that each part may be attached to the canoe with the use of a screwdriver and a pair of pliers.

A lateen, or triangular-shaped, sail is used. Units with a 45 square-foot sail are ideal for canoes up to 15 feet long. A 65 square-foot sail is recommended for canoes over 15 feet long.

It is best to buy your sailing unit from the manufacturer of your canoe. Then all parts will be properly fitted and sure to function efficiently. Your canoe dealer can help you to select the correct sailing unit and can supply plans and instructions for its installation and use.

Another variation of canoeing involves the fabric-hulled collapsible foldboat. Especially popular in Europe, the foldboat is widely used in the United States for white-water canoeing. Because it draws only three inches of water, it can skim rapidly over the surface of the swift, foamy rivers and streams known as white waters.

You can convert your canoe into a jaunty sailboat by attaching leeboards, a rudder, and a double lateen sailing rig.

The foldboat is assembled by locking together the numbered parts of the frame. The fore and aft portions are then inserted into the rubberized canvas hull, and secured to make a drum-tight, streamlined craft. During transportation and storage, the parts are contained in two duffel bags.

Models range in length from the one-seat 14-footer to the two-seat 18-foot boat that can carry 600 to 700 pounds. The weight of the average foldboat is 50 pounds.

In the foldboat, the paddler sits on the seat or cushion and extends his legs. He uses a double-bladed paddle, dipping it first on one side and then on the other in alternating strokes. Although essentially a paddling craft, the foldboat also can be sailed or propelled with a small outboard motor.

Inflatable craft provide a third specialized form of canoeing. They are especially popular in those parts of the United States where the waters are fast, rock strewn, and turbulent.

Made of fabric and lacking a heavy frame, inflatable boats and canoes are easily transported to the water's edge. There they can be quickly unpacked and inflated with a hand or foot pump. Blowing up their large air chambers with lung power is impossible.

The inflatable fabric canoe, used to shoot rapids and run swift water, is constructed of synthetic rubber that is electronically welded to withstand collision, sun, salt water, and chlorine. When inflated, it has pointed ends and slanted sides. The streamlined craft bounces off rocks like a rubber ball, providing a sporty ride in comparative safety. Inflated floors, seats, and backrests contribute to the safety, as does the fact that a puncture in one of the canoe's several air chambers will not deflate the entire craft.

The inflatable canoe is propelled by a paddler using a double-bladed paddle. He sits on the canoe's centerline and alternately dips the blades on either side of the craft. One or two paddlers may be employed, depending on whether the canoe is a single-

Because of their ability to bounce off obstructions, inflatable canoes are used frequently for white-water canoeing.

or double-seat model. A wide range of canoe sizes is available, ranging from 4 feet, 4 inches to 11 feet.

The Eskimo's contribution to present-day watercraft is the kayak, a very narrow, sharp-ended, skin-covered canoe. A wide variety of designs was originally found among the various tribes, but nearly all had these basic characteristics: ease of paddling, speed, maneuverability, lightness in weight, and the ability to work against strong winds, tides, and heavy seas.

The modern kayak has the same sleek design, covered deck, and small cockpit as the original sealskin craft of the Eskimos. The kayaks above are: (left) a folding craft and (right) a rigid one-piece model.

In general, the kayak is made for a single occupant, who sits on the bottom with his head and upper body protruding through a hole or cockpit opening. Propulsion is supplied by a double-bladed paddle from six to seven feet long. The kayak is so light that it can be carried like a large basket by inserting one arm under the decking at the cockpit opening.

Modern canoeists have created two basic versions of the kayak—the rigid and the collapsible. Instead of the Eskimo's driftwood or willow framework, today's hulls are made of plywood; specialized fabrics have replaced the original sealskin, and sturdy mahogany is used to frame the cockpit.

This sleek craft is ideal for running the wildest water in a sporting challenge of man against nature. So exciting is kayaking that kayak racing is included in the Olympic Games.

CHAPTER TWO

PADDLES AND OTHER EQUIPMENT

The methods of making a canoe move are varied. It can be paddled, poled, sailed, or pushed along with the aid of an outboard motor. However, the main source of power for a canoe is paddling.

PADDLES   The paddle is probably your most important piece of canoeing equipment. It should be selected with care, and once owned, it should be treated properly.

PARTS OF A PADDLE

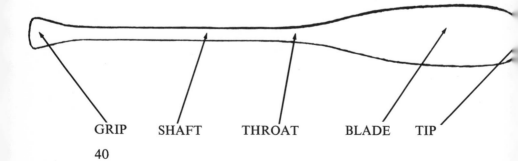

GRIP   SHAFT   THROAT   BLADE   TIP

Although all paddles look generally alike, there are variations in the shape and size of the blade, the style of the grip, and the length of the shaft. The relationship in size of blade to shaft is proportionately the same for all paddles.

One of the most popular blade shapes is the oval beaver tail. The short blade with rounded tip is recommended for beginners because it is easier to pull through the water and is not too heavy.

Other blade shapes are generally of specialized design, construction, size, or use. The Indian paddle has a narrow blade, which is ideal for short, steady, tireless strokes. The laminated racing paddle, with its wide blade and square tip, bites solidly into the water, and is recommended only for strong paddlers. Ranging between these two shapes are such other paddle designs as Maine Guide, Riedel, Sugar Island, Samoset, and Voyageur. In addition, there is the double-bladed paddle, which has a long shaft with

A wide variety of paddle blades are manufactured to suit canoeists' personal tastes and all types of waterways.

a blade at each end. This paddle is used largely by expert canoeists for solo paddling and for propelling kayaks and foldboats.

More important than the design of a paddle blade, however, is the blade size. The proper size of blade depends upon the size and strength of the paddler. A blade that is too large for a paddler will be difficult to push through the water and will make paddling hard work. A blade that is too small will require faster stroking to control the canoe.

Paddle grips are available in two main styles— the pear grip and the T grip. As its name indicates, the pear grip has a rough triangular, or pear, shape. One of its biggest advantages is that it can be shaved down to fit the hand comfortably if it is too large when purchased. The T grip cannot be altered in this way, but some canoeists find it more comfortable and secure than the pear grip.

Paddles come in many lengths, and there are almost as many rules for determining the proper length for an individual canoeist. One flexible rule states that the paddle length should equal the ap-

Double-bladed paddles vary in shape, length, and construction. They are also designed with right-handed and left-handed control, so a canoeist must buy the control style appropriate for him.

proximate height of the user. However, arm-stretch span varies among individuals of the same height, so paddle length should vary, too. The beginner can avoid confusion by selecting a paddle long enough to allow him to submerge the entire blade when stroking, without having to lean over the side of the canoe and reach awkwardly. The stern paddler, who steers the canoe, should have a paddle measuring about two inches beyond his height. You will have to experiment with paddles of various lengths and grips to find the one best suited to your needs and abilities.

Factory-made paddles usually will be satisfactory for the beginner. Generally, they are constructed from one piece of hardwood, such as maple or ash. The natural strength of hardwood makes possible one-piece, mass-produced paddles. They are often thick, heavy, and prone to warping, but can be shaved down to give them a whippier quality. The ash paddle is slightly lighter than its maple counterpart, and is less likely to warp. In selecting a paddle, examine the wood for smooth grain, without

Paddle grips are available in an assortment of styles, including (left to right): T grip, Maine Guide grip, and two varieties of the pear grip.

knots or wavering lines.

Expert canoeists prefer paddles that are made from soft wood, like spruce, fir, cedar, or basswood. They are seldom made of only one piece, but are hand crafted by gluing several pieces of wood together in a strong laminated construction. These paddles are extremely light and whippy and are ideal for open water.

Canoe paddles range in price from $4 for the four-foot size to $5.50 for the five-footer. Paddles of specialized shapes, laminated construction, and light, resilient wood cost more.

Good canoeists take pride in their paddles, and provide them with proper care and handling. The first step in paddle maintenance is to select an unpainted paddle and then to rub hot linseed oil into the blade and the shaft. Follow the Northwoods guides' practice of applying coat after coat of oil until the paddle will absorb no more. Then give the paddle a coat of shellac or varnish. When thoroughly dry, sandpaper it with a fine grain of paper, and apply a second coat of shellac or varnish. A hard finish on the grip will cause slipping and blistering; therefore, keep it bare and smooth by sanding it periodically.

Because of their importance and delicate construction, paddles should never be abused. They should not be used as hammers, frog swatters, or weapons in water fights. Neither should they serve as poles, for shoving off from rocks or sandbars frequently damages blades or snaps shafts. Besides, poling can be dangerous. If the blade slips off a rock or sticks in the mud, the paddler may fall into the water, lose the paddle, or capsize the canoe.

When not in use, paddles should be placed upright against a tree or other support. They should never be laid on the ground where they can be stepped on and broken. A serious canoeist also makes a special effort not to leave his paddles out in the hot sun where the heat will warp them. The thin-bladed paddle face is too delicate, and its function too important, to be endangered.

For winter storage, the paddle again should be stored upright, rather than flat. It is best to hang it up in a cool place. A screw eye in the top of the paddle grip will fit over a nail in a garage or basement wall.

It is wise to take a spare paddle on all canoe trips. Then if a paddle is lost or damaged, you will not be stranded.

SEAT CUSHIONS AND KNEE PADS   Many canoes today are equipped with a bow seat and a stern seat made of wood, woven cane, or aluminum. The comfort of these seats can be increased by padded seat cushions, which cost about $4. For a third passenger, you may add a folding crew seat made of canvas stretched over an aluminum frame. These light, comfortable seats sell for approximately $10.

Paddling a canoe from a kneeling position requires protection for the knees. Good kneeling pads can be made of a seat cushion, household kneeling pads of double thickness, basketball knee guards, a canvas bag, a hot-water bottle, or a pillowcase filled to puffiness with granulated cork, sponge rubber, sawdust, or kapok. An emergency pad may be a folded sweater, a heavy shirt, or canvas shoes, though wearing apparel should be used only in emergencies.

The most pressure on a pad is on the paddling side, so special protection should be placed there. When not in use, the kneeling pads are stowed in the ends of the canoe.

OTHER EQUIPMENT In addition to paddles and cushions, many pieces of equipment are available for canoeing. Some items are essential for safety and comfort. Others are luxury items that make the canoe more elegant or the sport more leisurely.

One necessary piece of equipment is rope, or line. For control of your canoe in towing, 30 to 50 feet of ⅜-inch Manila line should be attached to

You will cruise in comfort with such accessories as crew seats, cushions, backrests, and kneeling pads.

both the bow and stern of the canoe. Metal loops on the bow and stern ends, or holes in the decking, are provided for anchoring the line.

Another essential is a bailer. Every time you board a canoe, be absolutely sure a bailing device is stowed at the sternman's feet or in the point of the canoe. A tin cup or can, a plastic cup, a plastic detergent bottle with the bottom cut off, or a large sponge may be used to bail out the water that often accumulates in the bottom of the canoe. The efficient canoeist never allows such accumulations from leaks or high waves. He knows that water swishing back and forth in the canoe will soon soak the cargo and the feet of paddlers and passengers, and will affect control of the canoe.

An accessory that helps a single canoeist to transport a canoe comfortably is the carrying yoke. On one-man carries, the canoe is hoisted overhead and is supported on the canoeist's shoulders, with his hands grasping the gunwales. The yoke fits over his shoulders and cushions them against the pressure of the canoe. Most yokes are made of foam rubber pads covered with canvas or thick vinyl and attached to a crosspiece of hard wood. They are fastened to the gunwales of the canoe at the point of balance whenever there are portages, or overland hikes from one body of water to another.

Pontoons are a specialized accessory based on an idea that was born centuries ago. At that time South Sea Islanders and American Indians along our ocean coasts tried to make their frail crafts more stable by attaching outriggers to their narrow boats, canoes, and dugouts. Their outriggers consisted of two large timbers, rigged to each side of the craft, a few feet from the hull. The timbers floated and supported the craft, thus preventing it from tipping.

Today we call these floating supports pontoons. Most are made of ethafoam plastic, balsa wood, or hollow cylinders, and have pointed or rounded ends. With these added stabilizers, canoeists can carry loads and can fish and hunt from their crafts with little worry about stability. A set of pontoons is particularly useful in large and rough waters, for they make a canoe practically tip-proof. Inquiry about pontoons should be made to the company that built your canoe, because it is best to use pontoons designed specifically for your canoe.

Canoes can be made more comfortable and plush-looking with the addition of such items as slat backrests, lazy-back cushion seats, floorboards, and canvas crew seats for passengers. All canoe manufacturers feature these accessories as well as outboard motor brackets, sailing rigs, and cartop carriers. Write to the manufacturer of your canoe if you want information about accessories.

With the recent surge in outboarding, the outboard motor has been added to the list of equipment available for canoeing. Many canoeists are now using small 1½- to 3-horsepower motors to give them a wider range of travel and to eliminate some of the strain of paddling. The cumbersome motor and the weight of the gasoline offer little burden if the canoe trip involves few portages.

Recognizing the popularity of the outboard motor, manufacturers now produce canoes with a square stern so that the motor can be easily attached. Square-stern models are available in nearly all sizes.

When outboard canoeing, a person familiar with the motor should be the skipper, for motorized power greatly affects a craft's balance and safety.

The square-stern canoe is designed so that you can attach a small outboard motor and enjoy the fun of power boating.

CHAPTER THREE

PADDLING TECHNIQUES

Watching a paddling demonstration or reading a canoeing book will help you become acquainted with stroking. Such preparation will enable you to understand the reasons for each propelling or controlling action. It is through continual practice, however, that you will develop the smoothly flowing movements of a good paddler.

DOCK OR POOLSIDE PRACTICE   Lead-up drills will introduce you to the basic techniques of paddling. For these drills, stand alongside an elevated backyard pool or practice from a pier, dock, or poolside that is not too far above the surface of the water.

First you must learn to handle the paddle correctly. The following instructions assume you will be paddling on the right side. When you paddle on the left side, change *right* to *left*, and vice versa. Hold the paddle grip with your left hand, knuckles on top, thumb on the right. This is like putting your fingers around a baseball. With your right hand, hold the shaft of the paddle at the throat, just above the blade. Now you are ready to begin the drills.

Hold the paddle with your upper hand firmly over the grip and your lower hand around the throat.

Drill Number 1 involves the elements of the bow stroke. It will help you get the feel of the paddle as it strokes water. You will discover how water pressure resists paddle action as you stroke.

1. Stand with your right hip touching the edge of the pool, or if you are at a dock, kneel sideways near the water.

2. Hold the paddle forward over the water, as far as your arms can reach, in a vertical, or upright, position. The blade edges should point sideways. Your left hand remains chin high.

3. Dip the blade straight down into the water, but make sure your extended right hand stays on the paddle throat, above the surface of the water.

4. Push forward with your left hand to make the paddle blade swing backward in a slight arc toward your hip. Notice how difficult this movement is against the resistance of the water.

POSITION FOR POOLSIDE DRILLS

5. Now, keeping the paddle blade in the water, reverse the action. Push your right hand forward as you pull backward with your left arm until the blade reaches its original position in the water. Feel how this pushing motion strains your muscles.

6. Repeat this back-and-forth motion without removing the paddle from the water. In this action are the essentials of both the bow and the backwater stroke.

Drill Number 2 demonstrates the ease with which a paddle on edge slashes or slices through the water.

1. Hold your paddle as instructed in Drill Number 1. Stand poolside in the same way. Lower the blade into the water, as far forward as your arms can comfortably reach. Turn the blade so that the edges point forward and backward.

2. Push your left hand and arm forward while your right hand acts like a pivot, slicing the blade underwater in an arc toward your hip.

3. With the blade still in the water, reverse the action. Push your right arm forward on the throat and pull your left arm and hand backward to your starting point. This movement is quite easy because there is little water resistance.

4. Repeat this simple water-cutting action.

Drill Number 3 illustrates how water pressure tends to move an angled blade away from you and out of control.

1. Stand poolside holding the paddle as directed in Drill Number 1.

2. After you dip the blade forward into the water, turn it clockwise so that the edge near you moves forward until it slants away from you at an angle of approximately 45 degrees, or ⅛ of a circle.

3. With your right hand holding the throat, your left arm pushes forward with the grip, away from your chin. The angled blade sweeping through the water will have a tendency to ride away from you toward the center of the pool.

4. You will find this maneuver fairly difficult. Practice it repeatedly. Force the blade to follow a path toward you, even though the angled position of the blade will tend to move it away from you.

5. Then reverse the drill, with the paddle on the same angle, but opposite your hip. Push the blade forward with your right arm, while your left hand pulls backward on the grip. This reverse action will tend to drive the blade toward the edge of the pool.

Drill Number 4 helps you learn how to turn the paddle to complete a stroke. The J stroke requires such turning.

1. Repeat the first four steps in Drill Number 1.

2. As you near the end of the stroke, when the paddle is opposite your hip, turn the blade counterclockwise, the inner edge toward the back. By flexing your wrists, continue turning the paddle toward the rear until a quarter-circle arc, or 90 degees, is reached. The blade will now be parallel with the side of the pool, as in the slicing drill.

3. A final push outward from the canoe gives a rudder action that steers the canoe. This curved tail of the path of the blade on edge at the end of the stroke permits easy removal of the paddle from the water.

As you practice all of these drills, you will become acquainted with the power needed to execute actual strokes. At the same time, you will be strengthening the muscles used in paddling.

PADDLING IN A CANOE While learning the skills of canoeing, do not go out on the water alone. Always take a companion. If possible, go with an experienced canoeist who will direct, analyze, and constructively criticize your paddling techniques. If you cannot obtain such instruction, choose a paddling companion who can watch for your faults. In either case, you should wear a life jacket in the canoe, and you should know how to swim or at least how to stay afloat.

Begin your paddling sessions with a partner on a small shallow lake or slow-moving stream. The two of you should stroke rhythmically together on opposite sides of the canoe. At first make short runs along the shore. After a few sessions, you will be stronger and better skilled and will be able to stay out for a longer time.

In the beginning, position yourself in the bow of the canoe, with your fellow paddler in the stern. This will enable you to learn the bow strokes, used primarily to move the canoe forward. Later you can progress to the stern position, where the steering strokes are executed. The bow position, with only a few feet of canoe ahead of you, gives you a feeling of confinement. It is different from the stern position, with ten or more feet of stable craft looming securely in front of you.

Once stationed in the bow, you may paddle from either a sitting or a kneeling position. Although some experts recommend only the kneeling position, many canoeists find that they are able to handle the canoe efficiently, safely, and far more comfortably from the sitting position. Certainly it is easier for most beginners to learn paddling while seated on the bow seat. The thwarts must never be used as seats, for the high seating position affects balance, and a sudden lurch or high wave will topple a person.

The kneeling position was, of course, used by those expert paddlers, the American Indians. They knelt while paddling to obtain better control, stability, safety, and stroking power. The paddler who sits erect on a canoe seat places all the strain on his arm and shoulder muscles. The kneeling paddler uses his arms and shoulders plus his back and thigh muscles, which require less exertion, while gaining more speed.

In the customary kneeling position, the paddler places his knees 12 to 18 inches apart on the pad on the floor of the canoe. He rests on his heels and braces his backside against a thwart. This low position, be-

For the customary kneeling position, place both knees 12 to 18 inches apart on the protective pad.

sides having a muscular advantage and added stroking power, offers less resistance to the wind.

As a variation to the customary position, the paddler may kneel on one knee only, with the other leg extended forward. Braced in this way, he has three points of support: knee, extended leg, and body against the thwart. For paddling freedom and better stroking leverage, the knee on the paddling side is down, while the other leg is extended. To relieve muscle strain, the paddling side and the leg positions can be changed from time to time.

A third position, called the high-kneeling or racing-kneeling position, is used for speed. In this technique, the paddler does not lean back against a thwart or sit on his heels. He rests on one knee and brings the other leg up so that the shoe grips the

For the high-kneeling position, kneel on one knee, and bring up your other leg to balance your body in a raised, upright position.

floor of the canoe. This position, with the thigh and the trunk upright, raises the body to a high-kneeling position that gives excellent leverage to a stroke.

For safety and progress in solo paddling, kneeling is a must. The paddler can easily trim the canoe by moving fore or aft until the proper balance position is found. However, to reach the water effectively with the paddle from amidships, a slight tilt to the canoe is necessary. The paddler accomplishes this by taking a position slightly off center, toward the paddling side.

Even though paddling from the knees will probably cause preliminary discomfort, you should add the technique to your canoeing skills. Through practice, your body will become accustomed to the stresses of this paddling method, which produces great speed and efficiency when mastered.

In both the sitting and the kneeling positions, your posture should be essentially the same. Your back should be straight, your muscles relaxed, and your head held high. Turn your body slightly toward the water on your paddling side. Remain upright throughout each stroke, and do not sway your body. Your own comfort and the response of the canoe to your paddling will indicate whether you are in the proper position and are stroking correctly.

THE BOW STROKE The first strokes you should learn are the two strokes for propelling the canoe forward—the bow stroke and the J stroke. The bow stroke is the simpler one. It is a straight pull and power stroke executed from the bow of the canoe. It has little steering function.

The bow stroke, and most other strokes, can be performed on either the right or the left side. To cover both situations, the following instructions do not refer to the *right* hand or arm or the *left* hand or arm. Instead, the term *upper* is used to designate the hand and arm controlling the paddle grip, and *lower* to designate the hand and arm controlling the paddle throat.

For the bow stroke, assume your sitting or kneeling position in the bow of the canoe. Hold the paddle in the direction of the bow. Dip the paddle blade into the water close to the bow and at a right angle to the center line of the canoe. Keeping close to

THE BOW STROKE

your chin, thrust your upper arm diagonally forward like a boxer throwing a punch in slow motion. Your lower hand, acting as a moving fulcrum, or axle, permits the paddle to move through the water like a pendulum. It is this lever action that drives the canoe forward.

The blade's path should be parallel to the center line of the canoe and not to the curved side. However, perform this stroke as close as possible to the side of the canoe without scraping your hand, the paddle, or the gunwale of the canoe.

When the blade reaches a point opposite your hip, twist the paddle counter-clockwise, turning the blade face parallel to the keel. Push your upper arm downward and raise your lower hand to turn the blade out of the water in a splashless motion. Then, with the blade parallel to the water's surface, swing the paddle forward for the next stroke. Returning the paddle above and parallel to the water is called *feathering*. It cuts wind resistance on the forward blade action, and the blade skims over the waves on a windy day. The whole process of returning the paddle to the starting point of the next stroke is known as the *recovery*.

This simple paddle stroke sends the canoe surging forward with surprising ease. When mastered, its rhythmic sequence of dip, push, and recovery becomes a movement of beauty and grace.

THE J STROKE   When a paddler uses a straight bow stroke, there is a tendency for the canoe to veer slightly from a straight course. One reason for this is the position of the paddler's seat. To make room in the canoe for the bowman's feet, the bow seat is set back from the prow, or front tip. The stern seat is closer to the tip of the stern and farther from the wide center portion of the canoe. In straight stroking, the sternman's paddle sweeps toward the tapering end of the canoe and causes the bow end to veer to the opposite direction of the stroking stern paddler. The J stroke, mainly executed from the stern, counteracts this veering tendency and keeps the canoe on course. At the same time, it propels the canoe forward.

Begin the J stroke like the bow stroke, with your upper hand near your chin and your lower hand extending forward. Pull the paddle through the

THE J STROKE

water in the same straight pattern until your lower hand nears your hip. Then turn your upper hand counter-clockwise so that the blade edge curves toward the stern. Continue a gradual sweep away from the canoe, executing a rough J pattern in the water with the blade face.

Your upper hand should be pulling in as your lower hand pushes slightly outward to complete the J. The stroke ends with the blade face parallel to the side of the canoe. Slice the blade out of the water on edge. Then make the recovery, swinging the paddle forward parallel to the water.

Beginners have a tendency to bring the paddle shaft to the gunwale to pry the blade into a sweeping J finish. Some use the paddle as a rudder by trailing it in the water at the end of each stroke. Although they may seem easier, these practices greatly interfere with the canoe's smooth forward progress. The J stroke may be difficult at first, but it becomes smooth and natural with practice.

THE DRAW STROKES   To move a canoe sideways or to turn it to one side, two main types of strokes are used—the draw strokes and the sweep strokes.

The draw strokes give the beginner the ability to make a sharper turn than the other strokes. They are very useful, but are quite simple and can be mastered in a short time. The two basic strokes are the in-draw and the out-draw, sometimes called the pull-over and the push-over.

For better leverage on the in-draw, place your lower hand a few inches above the paddle throat. Extend the paddle far out into the water on a line with your hip. The blade should face the side of the canoe. Pull the paddle toward the canoe with your lower hand, and press outward with your upper hand. This action draws the side of the canoe toward the paddle. Quickly slice the paddle toward the stern and out of the water to prevent it from banging the canoe.

To move sideways, both the bow and the stern

THE IN-DRAW STROKE

THE OUT-DRAW STROKE

paddler execute the in-draw on the same side. When they execute it on opposite sides, the canoe pivots.

The out-draw stroke is the direct opposite of the in-draw. Place the blade in the water near and parallel to the side of the canoe. Push out with your lower arm, and pull across with your upper arm. At the end of the stroke, with the blade near the water surface, recover and feather as in the bow stroke. This stroke drives the canoe sideways away from the paddle.

THE SWEEP STROKES   In the second type of turning strokes, the sweep strokes, you use the paddle like an oar. Your upper arm should be bent, and your lower arm should be fairly straight and moved up on the paddle.

As bowman in tandem paddling, you perform the sweep in this way. Reach directly ahead to the bow and lightly dip the paddle at an angle into the water.

QUARTER SWEEP
FROM THE BOW

QUARTER SWEEP
FROM THE STERN

THE REVERSE
SWEEP

Then, holding the paddle almost horizontally, swing outward and backward through an arc of up to 90 degrees for a quarter sweep. This stroke turns the canoe away from the side on which you stroke. For a half sweep, used in solo paddling, the arc should be 90 degrees or more. A full sweep of the paddle back to the stern is very powerful and may turn the canoe too fast for a beginner to maintain proper control.

The reverse bow sweep is executed with action opposite that of the bow sweep. Begin with the paddle blade entering the water directly opposite your hip and sweep forward. This stroke turns the canoe toward the sweep side. The sternman performs a reverse sweep by dipping the paddle astern and sweeping the blade abeam.

When the bowman makes a regular sweep on one side and the sternman uses the reverse sweep on the other, the canoe pivots. The pivot is useful for maneuvering the canoe in a small area.

65

THE JAM STROKE   The jam stroke is a stopping stroke. It brakes the forward motion of the canoe. To execute it, slice the paddle blade downward into the water alongside the canoe. Keep the blade perpendicular to the keel. For support, hold the paddle with the thumb and fingers of your lower hand locked securely against the gunwale. Hold the grip firmly with your upper hand. To avoid tipping the canoe, the bowman and the sternman should perform the jam stroke in unison on opposite sides.

THE JAM STROKE

THE BACKWATER STROKE   To reverse, or back up, a canoe, the backwater stroke is used. This stroke is the opposite of the bow stroke. In backwatering, you must first brake the forward motion of the canoe. Then dip the paddle blade into the water opposite your hip, with the blade perpendicular to

THE BACKWATER STROKE

the center line of the canoe. Push the blade forward with your lower arm, and pull the grip backward with your upper arm. When you have pushed the paddle as far as you can, lift the blade from the water and swing the paddle toward the stern to begin the next stroke.

ADVANCED STROKES   There are many advanced strokes that require strength and experience, and should be attempted only after the basic strokes have been mastered.

The bow rudder stroke is important in avoiding hazards that only the bowman can see. Thus, he becomes a steersman, sharply turning the canoe from its course. The bow rudder stroke is not really a stroke, but a hold-paddle position. The blade is held in the water nearly perpendicular to the canoe. Its forward edge slants away from the bow at a slight angle. The trapped water between the bow and the paddle blade quickly turns the canoe toward the paddling side. The pressure of this water places much strain on the paddler. If there is strong momentum, the paddle can be wrenched out of his hand. To prevent this, the paddle can be braced against the gunwale to help hold it firm.

The cross bow rudder stroke is executed on the side opposite the bowman's paddling side. He swings his body quickly to that side and knifes the paddle blade into the water, holding it firmly in the same way as required for the bow rudder stroke. This maneuver turns the canoe away from the bowman's normal paddling side.

The sculling and reverse sculling strokes have many advantages in wildlife observation, for they keep the canoe steady and move it sideways. Sculling is concerned more with control than with speed. The paddle blade, held at an angle to the canoe, is kept in the water at all times. The face of the blade can be pulled back, pushed forward, or moved outward or inward. Recovery is always made by slicing the blade back to its original position. A little experimentation will enable the canoeist to learn the reaction of the canoe to these silent movements.

CHAPTER FOUR

HANDLING YOUR CANOE

As with paddle strokes, canoeists have definite ways of carrying the canoe, launching it, boarding it, cruising, and docking or landing. You must learn these methods so that you can handle your canoe in all situations—on land and water, on quiet lakes and rushing rivers, on afternoon outings and week-long trips.

CARRYING METHODS   Carrying the canoe to the water from the car, truck, or storage rack is the first activity. To avoid excessive strain on the crew members, and to prevent possible damage to the canoe, it is best to use two or more carriers. Canoes are damaged more frequently on dry land than in the water, so do not show off your strength or play around when carrying them.

One of the simplest canoe carries is the wedge, or deck, carry. With the canoe on the ground, right side up, the crew member at the bow end places his fingers under the curved edge of the wedge. The stern carrier, standing on the opposite side of the bow carrier, grasps backhanded under the stern wedge. Then, facing forward, the carriers lift together on signal and carry the canoe right side up.

The gunwale carry is very similar. Again the canoe is resting upright on the ground. The two carriers stand at the center, or point of balance, of the canoe, one on each side. They turn their bodies to face the bow, or direction of the carry. They bend down by flexing their knees and, with the hand near the canoe, hook their fingers under the inwale in a firm grip. Then, on signal, they lift. The balanced canoe remains parallel to the ground during the carry.

The gunwale carry can also be used by four persons. Two crew members stand by the bow seat, one on each side. The other two take gunwale positions near the stern seat. All crew members face the bow, standing sideways to the canoe. They grasp the inwales with the hands adjacent to the canoe, lift it together on signal, and proceed to the launching site. The canoe's weight, distributed over four points, makes the task of carrying quite easy.

For all of these carries, the paddles can be placed in the bottom of the canoe if the carry is short. For longer hauls, paddles, fishing poles, and other long items should be lashed to the thwarts.

A carrying method that should be used with caution is the one-man overhead carry. It should be attempted only if you are near-adult in size and

TWO-MAN WEDGE CARRY TWO-MAN GUNWALE CARRY

FOUR-MAN WEDGE CARRY

ONE-MAN OVERHEAD CARRY

strength, use a small, light canoe with a yoke, and have the help of a partner.

To get the canoe overhead, use the walk-up system. Have your partner lift one end of the upside-down canoe as you walk under it. Move forward, sliding your hands along the gunwales until you reach the point of balance, which is slightly ahead of center. As the canoe levels off, duck your head so that your shoulders are brought up under the yoke. Your shoulders and outstretched hands on the gunwales give a three-point support. Carry the canoe with its leading end slightly higher than the back for a better view of the path.

LAUNCHING AND BOARDING   The canoe should always be carried to the water for launching. Never drag, pull, push, or slide it along, for this can severely damage the bottom.

The procedure for launching from a level or gently sloping shore is known as beach launching. For this procedure, the stern of the canoe is usually dunked first. Therefore, it is best to use the two-man gunwale carry, which leaves the canoe ends free.

Approaching the water's edge with this carry, you and your fellow launcher should extend the stern over the water and gently lower the canoe toward it. Slide your hands back from the point of balance to dip the stern of the canoe. Keep sliding back on the gunwales, hand over hand, and feed the canoe into the water. Take care not to scrape the

From a level launching site, feed the canoe gently into the water so that the bottom does not scrape on sand or rocks.

bottom of the canoe on any sand or rocks that may damage it.

When afloat perpendicular to the shoreline, the canoe should have contact with the shore, with the bow lightly touching the sand bottom. The bowman steadies the canoe by bracing it between his knees in a straddling position. For additional control of the canoe during the sternman's boarding, the bowman also leans over and places his hands on the gunwales.

The sternman, with paddle in hand, steps around the bowman and enters the canoe by placing one foot in the center of the bottom. He bends over to grasp the gunwales, then brings in his other foot. Crouching so that his body stays low, he moves toward the stern of the canoe, sliding both hands along

When beach launching, the bowman steadies the canoe between his knees as the sternman carefully enters, keeping his body low and his hands on the gunwales.

the gunwales. During the forward movement, he keeps his toes slightly turned in for better balance. Once seated in the stern seat, he dips the paddle in the water to steady the canoe while the bowman enters.

The bowman, preparatory to boarding, lifts the bow free of the bottom. Then, with a slight push-off, he steps directly into the canoe, turns around, and sits down.

Should the canoe, with the added weight, remain in contact with the sand bottom, the bowman, hands on the gunwales, proceeds amidships. This shifts the trim of the canoe and makes it waterborne. Once the canoe is afloat, the sternman maneuvers it into deeper water. Then the bowman returns to his paddling position.

Launching a canoe from a dock, high bank, or rocky ledge is called dock, or alongside, launching. This type of launching offers more advantages than boarding from a beach, so always be on the lookout for situations that will allow it.

From a dock, the canoe's entry into the water is best accomplished by the two-man gunwale, hand-over-hand technique just explained. After the canoe is afloat, it is brought alongside, or parallel to, the dock. With the canoe floating in a sufficient depth of water, and the dock providing firm footing, duffel can be lowered into the canoe and passengers can board with ease.

If only two people are going out, the bowman generally boards first. To steady the canoe while the

In one method of dock launching, the carriers stand side by side, grasp one gunwale, and gently lower the canoe into the water, using the legs as guides.

bowman boards, the sternman kneels on the dock and grasps the near gunwale. The bowman kneels too, and facing the bow, moves the foot next to the canoe to the center of the canoe, the weight of his body resting on the foot that is still on the dock. This first step into the canoe should be executed with a downward pressure—not at an angle that will tend to push the canoe away. Quickly the bowman transfers his weight from the dock to the canoe as he brings his other foot aboard. Then, bending over, he grasps the gunwales and slides along, body low but head up, until he reaches his paddling position.

The sternman, following the same procedure, enters amidships and steps to his position. Some expert sternmen prefer to board first, so they can

In dock launching, the bowman boards, crouching low and grasping the gunwales, while the sternman holds onto the near gunwale.

keep an eye on the activity before them, while holding the canoe free from the dock. However, in most cases, the sequence should be bowman, then sternman.

If a third person is in the party, he should be the first to board for stabilizing reasons. His boarding procedure is the same as the bowman and sternman's.

Whether beach launching or dock launching, you must always enter the canoe with care—to protect yourself as well as your craft. Just as you should never step into the canoe when it is on the ground, never jump into it when it is in the water. Such treatment usually damages the canoe and may tip it, giving you a surprise dunking. Stepping on the gunwale may also cause damage or injury. Avoid missteps by following the boarding procedures carefully, always staying low in the canoe and moving slowly.

CRUISING   Once your canoe is afloat and free, you are ready to explore the coves, bays, and islands of your watery domain in ways that no other boat can. Shallow water, narrow creeks, boulders, and stumps offer no obstacle to your manueverable canoe as it cruises over and around the rough spots and snags.

However, as with all new experiences, approach your first cruises cautiously and gradually. First, try short trips along the shore. Then, as your ability and self-confidence grow, you may make cruises across small lakes and into bays, outlets, and slow, shallow streams. In this enlarged and challenging realm, you will experience the fun of controlling your canoe as you ride the waves. You will also discover how accurately you can plot and follow a course.

In preparation for extended cruising, rub a little vaseline, cream, or olive oil on your hands to prevent blistering. As your hands toughen, this will be unnecessary.

On extended trips, it is vitally important that you inform parents, friends, outfitter, or local ranger of your plans—your route, intended campsites, and approximate timetable. Then, if difficulties arise, people will know where to locate you.

Once the cruise is under way, the bowman sets the paddle-stroke pace. The Cree Indians in Canada execute 40 to 50 strokes per minute. Of necessity, they use short strokes. Without trying to match the Indians' pace, the beginning canoeist should make his strokes short, but regular. The stern paddler matches the pace set by the bowman and keeps the canoe on course, using the J stroke when and if necessary. When paddlers are well matched and the canoe rides on a straight course, the sternman uses a straight bow stroke.

Paddlers dip their blades and stroke in unison, so both must keep in mind that a steady pace—even if it is slow—is best. Avoid the beginner's urge to start out with a fast pace that cannot be continued.

Tandem paddling is the term for two paddlers stroking together. To maintain a smooth forward movement, the paddlers stroke on opposite sides of canoe.

Should the bowman become tired of paddling on one side, he can shift to the other by swinging his paddle over the bow, so that the blade covers a half circle in the air. No other signal is necessary. The stern paddler should automatically switch paddling sides to accommodate the bowman's change.

Throughout the cruise, the good canoeist, like the veteran outdoorsman, is constantly alert to weather signs, especially wind and wave conditions. Low fast-moving clouds, a sudden drop in temperature, wind shifts, and darkening skies are signs to stay ashore, to defer your cruise until favorable weather comes—and it always does if you wait it out. No cruise is important enough for you to risk the safety of yourself or your canoe by going out

78

during inclement weather. Remember, when you are far from shore, you are at the mercy of the elements, and they can be far stronger than men and boats.

Because the weather is not always ideal, learn to make the most of a bad situation. If forced to lay over for a while, use the time to fish on the leeward shore, repair gear, sew patches and buttons on clothes, or enjoy scuttlebutt sessions.

To minimize the effect of weather on your cruise, always keep as close as possible to land. Plot your paddling route so that islands, high bluffs, and points of land will furnish shelter from the wind. Taking advantage of these windbreaks sometimes requires a different, longer course than the most direct one, but the safety considerations make sense.

If a high wind does develop when you are in the middle of a lake, paddle immediately toward the nearest shore. Paddle steadily to control the canoe; don't let the wind dictate your course or speed. Stay low in the canoe to avoid tipping.

While paddling toward shore, do not permit the waves to hit your canoe broadside. Take them at an angle. This will prevent the waves from washing over the gunwales and swamping the canoe. The technique of slicing the waves at an angle of 45 degrees or less is called quartering. To reach your destination when quartering, you must follow a zigzag path, rather than a straight course. Quartering of waves may be done whether you are going upwind or downwind.

When you reach the shore, stay there until the wind dies down. Stay for an hour, four hours, overnight if necessary. Build a fire, and remain calm. You may be tired, wet, worried—but you'll be safe. By remaining in one place, it will be easier for searchers to find you. Remember that you will be missed, and help will arrive.

BEACHING AND DOCKING Very few cruises, of course, end in races against the wind and the rain. Most are far more calm and comfortable than that, ending in a leisurely landing at a quiet beach or dock.

When your cruise finishes at a beach or other level area, bring your canoe in with the bow leading at right angles to the shore. Approach the shore carefully and slowly to prevent scraping the bottom of the canoe on sand or pebbles.

As soon as the canoe makes contact with the shore or the lake bottom, the bowman steps out and pulls the bow onto the beach. The canoe should not be pulled up so far that the middle leaves the water, forming a bridge between the shore and the water. A suspended canoe is easily damaged. The bowman steadies the canoe by straddling it between his knees, as he did in the boarding procedure at the start of the trip. The sternman, bending over and sliding his hands along the gunwales, walks forward along the center of the canoe and steps out. Then, using the gunwale carry, both crewmen lift the canoe and remove it from the water.

Should your cruise end at a dock or pier, paddle slowly toward the dock, approaching at a slight angle to it. Ease the canoe over until it rests broadside to the landing platform. The sternman holds onto the dock as the bow paddler, also holding the dock for support, steps out. His step from the middle of the canoe is fast and shifts his weight quickly from the canoe to the dock.

The bowman then kneels on the dock, leans over, and grasps the near gunwale, steadying the canoe while the sternman steps out. When the canoe is unloaded, the stern is pushed out at right angles to the dock. Then the crew members pull up the canoe with the gunwale lift, careful not to scrape the bottom on the edge of the dock.

Your cruise over, you are well on your way to mastering the skills of canoeing. You have carried your canoe without damaging it or straining yourself. You have launched it, used various paddling strokes to propel it, concerned yourself with navigation and weather-watching, and then brought the canoe safely back to shore.

All of these skills will bring you enjoyment again and again. However, to guarantee this satisfaction, you must assume the responsibility for, and assure the safety of, yourself, your crew, and your cargo. This means you must know how to handle emergencies, and the biggest emergency in canoeing is capsizing.

CAPSIZING   Upsetting a canoe is a rare experience. Usually it is the result of showing off, carelessness, or disregard for the principles involved in proper balance when loading a canoe or cruising. If you follow proper procedures, you may well enjoy canoeing all of your life without once capsizing.

Nevertheless, it is wise to know how to handle yourself and your canoe should a capsizing ever occur. It is also wise to stage a capsizing in a safe, controlled situation. Then you can see how little danger is involved if you follow the right techniques, and you can practice these techniques until your reactions are almost automatic.

The most important rule to remember about capsizing is: Always stay with the canoe! The canoe will float—whether it is upside down or upright and filled with water. Whatever its condition, it will remain buoyant and will support all of the passengers it carried. Don't abandon it under any circumstances.

The simplest thing to do in a capsizing is just to hold onto the canoe. This is the procedure recommended for beginning canoeists. If the canoe is upright, you may easily hold onto the gunwales. If it is overturned, grasp the upturned keel amidships or the bow or stern line. You need not try to move the canoe if people are nearby and can come to your rescue, or if the wind will carry you to shore.

However, you can propel the canoe from your position in the water if you want to do so. Swim to the stern of the canoe, grasp the stern end, and float the canoe, bow first, to shore. Use a flutter or frog kick as you push the canoe along. Do not hurry. Take your time, and rest frequently.

A more difficult maneuver may be attempted if the capsized canoe remains right side up and has shipped, or taken on, little water. In this situation, you may reenter the canoe in the following manner. Work your way to the amidship position of the canoe. Grasp the near gunwale; then reach across with one hand to the far gunwale. Do a vigorous flutter kick and push down on the near gunwale to bring up your hips. Then, with a twist of your body, flop onto the canoe so that you are lying across both gunwales. Swing in your legs, and assume a sitting position. Bail out the water, and continue paddling.

In situations where the canoe is upside down or where it is upright but filled with water, the beginning canoeist should not attempt to right the canoe or to reenter and bail. These procedures are best left to veteran canoeists. The beginner should just hold onto the canoe and float it to shore.

Whether veteran or beginner, however, it is important not to panic if your canoe capsizes. Catch your breath after the unexpected plunge. Then survey the situation, determine the best technique to follow, and set about it calmly. By using good sense and proper care, you will be able to get yourself and your canoe to shore safely—perhaps even to continue your cruise.

CHAPTER FIVE

CANOEING SAFETY

A canoe is a safe, durable craft, but carelessness can cause accidents. Taking all necessary precautions to make your cruise safe is mature, responsible behavior. You will enjoy canoeing only if you know how to provide safety and comfort for yourself and your passengers.

CANOE BALANCE   Imagine a strong steel bar running the length of the canoe a few inches above the keel. The ends of the bar, extending beyond the bow and the stern, rest upon carpenter's sawhorses, holding the canoe's keel about three feet above the ground. In this setup, the bar acts as an axle and the canoe is upright and perfectly balanced. Any pressure on the sides of the canoe or any weight off-center disturbs this balance.

If you were to:

1. Push down on a gunwale amidships, the canoe would tilt.

2. Sit on one gunwale, the canoe would roll over and upset.

3. Board the canoe or place a heavy object off-center, the canoe would sway from its balanced position, spilling its passengers or cargo.

The canoe would tilt, but would not overturn if you were to:

1. Sit on the bottom, in the middle of the canoe.

2. Roll from side to side on the bottom of the canoe.

3. Lie in the bottom of the canoe and rock it like a hammock.

4. Kneel on both knees, straddling the keel line, and rock from side to side.

These theoretical experiments illustrate that properly balanced weight, low and in the center, will not endanger the stability of the canoe.

The stability of a large ship is maintained with the use of ballast, which is a heavy material, usually sand, kept in the bottom of the hull. In a canoe, the passengers and cargo are located centrally and act as the ballast. For stability in a loaded canoe, the weight should be distributed from side to side and from end to end so that the bow rides on the water slightly higher than the stern. Lay the heaviest cargo on the bottom and the lightweight cargo on the top.

Bowman, passenger, sternman, and cargo are properly distributed so that the bow rides on the water slightly higher than the stern.

Be careful not to overload the canoe. The free-board, or the space between the waterline and the gunwale, should be at least seven inches in smooth water and more in rough water.

SAFETY GUIDE

1. Take care of your canoe, paddles, and other equipment. Always repair even the slightest damage and replace equipment that you cannot restore to good condition. Store your canoe and paddles properly in a safe, dry place.

2. Learn and practice the paddling strokes so that you are confident in your ability to control the canoe. Avoid such foolish and careless behavior as taking dares and showing off.

3. When you are rested, you will be more alert. Plan your canoe trip so that you have time to relax. If you are tired, stop to rest. Accidents may happen to the fatigued canoeist.

4. Always take a referee's whistle on a cruise. If you are in genuine danger, use the universal signal of distress known by all outdoorsmen—three shots, three flares, three whistle blasts, or three signals of anything that can be seen or heard.

5. Stow in the canoe a first-aid manual and a first-aid kit packed in a waterproof container.

6. Never go on a canoe trip alone. If you go with a group, stay with them. If you should lose your way, remain calm. Don't wander aimlessly about. Stay where you can be seen.

7. Know basic swim techniques such as floating and treading water. Find out about instructions in water safety at your school, the Scouts, the YMCA and YWCA, the American Red Cross, or camps. Canoeists should always wear life jackets in a canoe, and one qualified swimmer should accompany each non-swimmer.

8. Do not panic if your canoe should capsize. Always stay with a capsized canoe. Kicking the boat to shore or waiting for someone to come for you is easier than emptying the canoe and trying to re-board.

9. Be alert for weather and water danger signals. Postpone or delay your trip during high winds and storms. If you are caught in a storm, head directly toward the shore, where you should take cover if possible. Stay away from trees, hills, and wire fences, for they may attract lightning. When the water becomes rough and you cannot control your canoe, go ashore until the condition subsides. Water is calmest in the early morning and around sunset.

10. Do most of your fishing from rocky shores. There the footing is good, and you can cover a wide area by casting. Should you fish while in the canoe, remember the principles of balance. Do not lean over to play a hooked fish. Let the rod do the work as you keep to the center line of the canoe. If you make the fish fight the rod, eventually the fish will be subdued and calm enough for netting.

11. Should you decide to stop for a swim, paddle the canoe to a sandy beach, carry it ashore, and then go swimming. Never dive from a canoe, for you could upset the canoe or injure yourself. Also, the wind can blow away an empty canoe so that not even an Olympic swimmer could catch up with it.

12. Plan your canoe outing carefully even if you are out for only a few hours. Each time you go out, check your canoe and paddles and take note of water and weather conditions. If you are going on a long trip, find out about the area, have plenty of maps, and outline the activities for each day.

CHAPTER SIX

CANOE-CAMPING TRIPS

Canoeing is gaining more devotees each year. Among the 10 million young people who go to summer camp, many attend camps devoted exclusively to canoeing. Their program starts with group instruction; then campers spend the rest of the summer on water trails with canoe-camping experts. Each camp has its own tests for qualification to take extensive trips. If you are interested in such a camp, find out its requirements and work on them in order to qualify for a summer of canoeing fun.

Many general summer camps, Scout groups, and other organizations also include canoe-camping in their programs. And more and more young people are enjoying the activity with their families on vacations. If you plan to go canoe-camping with such a group or with your family, it is wise to practice your canoeing skills in advance, so you won't be out of condition for the trip.

You may already have camping experience. If you have gone on a car-camping trip, you no doubt took a heavy tent, cot, mattresses, cookstove, and other equipment. The canoe-camping trip is different. It requires that all essential equipment be lightweight and that all supplies for the trip be carried within the canoe, and on the back when portaging. There is no chance to call anyone to help meet an emergency; there are no supermarkets along the waterways to supplement daily needs. You are completely on your own.

Knowledge of outdoor skills and thorough advance planning contribute to satisfying camping experiences. Many books devoted only to camping are available to help you gain this knowledge and planning ability. You should read several to get more detailed information on camping equipment and techniques than can be provided here.

Besides reading about camping, you should also practice camping, especially when canoeing is involved. Don't take a long trip until you have made some preliminary trips and experienced an overnighter or two. These short test-run trips, across a lake or a portion of a small river, will give you added information about your craft, your equipment, and your personal needs. Test runs also provide experience in loading your cargo and setting up your camp. Most important of all, they give you an opportunity to revise your equipment list and plans for an extended trip.

In making preliminary trips, as well as longer trips, set up your camp only in approved places. Do not camp on private property or restricted areas without permission.

PLANNING YOUR TRIP   Plan your extended canoe trip with great care. The first questions to be answered are: where shall we go, how long shall we stay, and what shall we do—explore, go sight-seeing, swim, snorkel, fish, visit remote Indian villages? The locale will, of course, determine the activities.

There are many patches of wilderness that can

Careful handling of your canoe and use of the proper equipment will provide a satisfying camping experience.

be reached only by canoe. Many states publish water routes and prepare campgrounds with cooking grills and sanitary facilities. They mark portage trails connecting different bodies of water and clear them of fallen trees and debris. (See Chapter Seven: Water Routes and Map Sources.)

Find out all you can about your chosen area. Get in touch with people who have been there. Write for information regarding the availability of rental canoes, equipment, food, required permits and licenses, and reservations if necessary.

As soon as possible, get a map of the area. Study it carefully for take-out locations; the nature of the water (large, open lakes or narrow streams); the number and length of portages; the number and size of islands (often ideal campsites, free from porcupines and pesky bears); and alternate routes (in case the one you choose should prove to be impractical).

NECESSARY EQUIPMENT Much of the success of canoe-camping depends upon having the necessary equipment for safety, comfort, and convenience. You need not own a complete outfit. Canoe-camping areas are sprinkled with outfitters who rent all of the gear you need for shelter, sleeping, and eating.

The following sections are intended as a brief guide to necessary camping equipment. For more details about each item, study some of the compre-

Pop tent, sleeping bags, and other camping equipment fit into duffel bags and rucksacks, which can be carried on a packboard.

hensive camping handbooks and catalogs of companies that serve Scouts, hikers, mountain climbers, and fishermen.

The tent is your home on a canoe-camping trip. Although seemingly fragile, it is a safe structure providing all the protection needed. The modern tent, properly pitched, or erected, will withstand wind and rain and be as satisfactory as a cabin. It is light in weight, easily set up and taken down, and better than the old heavy canvas models that require tent poles and stakes.

Two small tents are better than one large tent. Large tents are too bulky and heavy to pack and carry, and tent sites for them are difficult to find. Ideal for two or three persons is the 6′ x 9′ tent that weighs only 12 to 15 pounds and rolls into a small pack. Tents should have a built-in floor, zippered storm and mosquito-netting doors or flaps, and for cross ventilation a netted window that can be opened or closed from the inside.

Before a trip, set up your tent in the backyard to check it for leaks and tears. Be sure that rope and all other needed parts are there. Determine the available floor space by placing all gear inside, and check the sloping sides for head room. Don't worry too much about crowding the tent. Filled to capacity, it will provide warm sleeping.

The sleeping bag will provide warm sleeping, too. It maintains a uniform thickness of protection around the sleeper's body and has a waterproofed bottom to separate him from the damp ground. The ideal bag has a zipper or snaps all along one side and across the bottom, and a draft-free closure at the shoulders as well as around the face. In addition, it is light in weight and compresses into a small bundle for packing and transporting.

Sleeping bags of down, or duck feathers, best meet the requirements of cold temperatures and are the most expensive type. The second-best type, adequate for summer camping, is made of synthetic-polyester fiberfill, a tough material that is lightweight, warm, and mildewproof. Other sleeping bag materials include nylon, which is tough and quick-drying, and cotton, which, when kept dry, insulates as well as wool.

94

Removable outer cloth coverings and inner liners may be used to keep your sleeping bag clean and to prolong its life. Additional protection from ground coldness and dampness can be secured by using an inflatable air mattress. Good ones are made of rubberized nylon with a waffle pattern or of foam rubber, which insulates better, but is bulkier to pack. Should your sleeping gear be inadequate for an unseasonable drop in temperature, more warm clothing, like sweatshirts and slacks, may be donned.

Packsacks are essential for storing all necessities on a canoe trip. Packs are stowed in the bottom of the canoe when cruising and are carried overland when portaging. What comprises an ideal pack depends largely on individual preference.

The Boy Scout knapsack is, with variations, the most popular. It is made of heavy duck canvas, with two shoulder straps. A spacious container with a large open top and flap cover, it is easily packed and convenient for toting clothing and food. Some models have pockets for carrying small equipment.

Other packs that should be included if necessary are the Duluth packsack, with its greater load capacity; the pack basket, for toting hardware and canned goods; and the packboard, used to carry awkward or uncomfortably shaped loads.

Aluminum cooking kits are a great camping convenience. They contain a complete four-camper set of pots, frying pan, cups, plates, and utensils that fit completely into the outside pot for easy packing.

However, the cups in most kits conduct heat and burn the lips when hot beverages are served. Substitute enamel or stainless steel cups. After using, the kit should be packed in a heavy canvas bag with a drawstring, so that the blackened outside of the large pot will not smudge other duffel.

The pots, pans, and utensils of an aluminum cooking kit fit together for easy packing and storage. The lid of the large pot doubles as a frying pan.

Additional kitchen utensils, tools, accessories, personal items, and first-aid needs are listed on the following camping checklists. Use these lists as equipment guides, adding or subtracting items to meet your individual requirements.

CAMPING CHECKLISTS

KITCHEN UTENSILS

Can opener • Dishpan • Soap • Spatula • Dishcloths
Scouring pads • Plastic bucket • Heavy-duty knife
Washbasin • Dishtowels • Plastic bags
Long-handled ladle • Canvas storage bag

TOOLS

Axe with sheath • Nails • Twine • Folding shovel
Hone • Copper or aluminum wire • Wire-cutter pliers
Canvas storage bag • Screwdriver • File

ACCESSORIES

Flashlights • Canoe repair kit • Mosquito netting
Flashlight bulbs and batteries • Waterproofed maps
Binoculars • Pocketknives • Sewing kit
Waterproofed matches • Compass

PERSONAL ITEMS

Face soap • Washcloth and towel • Handkerchiefs
Toothbrush and paste • Clothespins • Toilet paper
Steel mirror • Extra shoelaces • Pencils and notebook
Razor and blades • Sunglasses • Referee's whistle
Chapstick • Skin lotion • Snippers • Swimsuit
Playing cards or other amusement • Candles

FIRST-AID KIT

First-aid manual • Surgical scissors • Adhesive tape
Iodine, Merthiolate, or Mercurochrome • Alcohol
Adhesive bandages • Thermometer • Sterile gauze
Elastic bandage • Calamine lotion • Sunburn lotion
Petroleum jelly or other burn ointment • Salt tablets
Water-purifying tablets • Aspirin or other pain-killer
Diarrhea and constipation medicines • Cotton swabs
Toothache drops • Personal prescription medicines
Insect repellent • Antacid • Cold tablets • Tweezers
Oral antibiotic • Snakebite kit • Antihistamine
Sulfa powder • Razor blades • Bug bomb

PROPER CLOTHING   Canoe-camping requires
little specialized clothing. Your regular sport or
leisure-time apparel is probably suitable. Just be sure
it is sturdy and comfortable, allows freedom of
movement, is loosely woven to permit rapid evapo-
ration of perspiration, and is washable.

Regular sport or work trousers that are sturdy,
have reinforced seams, deep roomy pockets, and a
buttoned opening are ideal for male campers. Accept-
able fabrics include denim, twill, cotton sateen,
water-repellent poplin, and wool and synthetic
blends. Favorites among girls and women are fron-
tier-style jeans of heavy denim and sanforized cotton
jeans with a concealed side zipper. Trousers and
jeans should be large enough to allow for tucking in

98

heavy shirts, thick underwear, and light sweaters. Be wary of stylish-looking sport clothes that will be impractical on the trail.

Camping shirts should have long sleeves for protection against cold, insects, and sunburn; two breast pockets with button-down flaps; and long tails to allow body exertion without popping out. Recommended fabrics include cotton chamois, army twill, soft synthetics, and fine wool, which is ideal but expensive. Shirts for female campers should also be long-sleeved, deep-pocketed, and made of sturdy cotton, washable wool and cotton, or wool flannel.

Canoe-campers need warm, durable clothing, sturdy shoes, and roomy packsacks.

For warmth, comfort, and practicality, nothing beats a loose long-sleeved soft wool sweater. Second-best is a long-sleeved turtleneck pullover made of heavy-nap cotton. Sweatshirts are adequate if the weather is dry and mild. Should the weather turn very chill, a lightweight, wind-proof, water-repellent jacket of tight-woven nylon or dacron worn over a wool shirt or sweater will supply adequate comfort without the bulk and weight of a heavy coat.

Two kinds of shoes should be taken on most canoe-camping trips. For wear inside the canoe, especially wood-canvas models, tennis shoes are recommended, for they do not scuff the floor ribs and planking. They also can be dried out by hanging them upside down on a line should they become wet. For portaging and general hiking, sturdy shoes of unlined leather are needed. These should be warm, offer firm support, and have arched inner soles and non-skid bottoms. Ankle-high and Oxford-style shoes with rustproof eyelets are recommended. Open-topped boots and loose-fitting loafers give little support, are slippery when wet, and do not fit snugly enough for sure-footed activity. Your walking shoes should be roomy enough to allow for two pairs of socks, and should be broken in before a trip. Protect them with a coating of wax-type boot grease.

Wool socks are ideal for camping. Soft, springy, and warm, they retain their quality through many launderings. If wool irritates you, wear a pair of cotton socks under the wool. For real comfort, include wool-cotton or wool-synthetic blends. Be sure your socks fit properly, because oversized socks that bunch at the toes and heels can cause blisters.

Underwear made of smooth cotton or fine wool is best for active canoe-campers. For many reasons, avoid synthetic fibers and abbreviated, binding styles. Thermal and fishnet underwear are excellent. Hollows in the weave of the cloth trap the air and insulate the body against cold. These undergarments are adaptable enough to be worn under pajamas on cold nights.

Raingear is necessary for protection against rain and against spray in the canoe. Although regular raincoats and hats are adequate, the best and most versatile piece of raingear is the hooded poncho. This rectangular-shaped garment slips over your head and drapes around your body, with openings on the sides. When under way, the poncho can be used to cover duffel in the canoe; and when on shore, it can cover packs at night, serve as a ground cloth under a sleeping bag, or provide a rug for lounging around the campfire.

Some kind of headgear is essential to ward off the hot sun or a cold wind on open water in a canoe. An old felt hat with a brim; a sailor's cap, turned down all around; a knitted navy watch cap, which can be rolled up or down over the ears as needed; or a beret or tam provide good protection against sun and rain. In addition, they can be folded and easily stowed in packsacks when not in use.

FOOD FOR THE TRIP   Food for a canoe-camping trip must meet strict requirements regarding weight and bulk. Today a wide variety of foods are dehydrated, concentrated, powdered, and freeze-dried to provide lightweight, compact foods that campers will find nutritious and tasty. Such specially processed foods are being stocked by more and more neighborhood supermarkets. If, however, you are unable to fill your needs at your local store, go to a camping supply store, or write one of the several mail-order firms specializing in lightweight camping foods; they will be glad to send you a list of their products.

To make food lightweight, of course, all water is removed. Therefore, you must add water when you prepare the food for eating. Follow the instructions on the food package, adding water until the item regains its original form. Prepare instant rice and potatoes with hot water, without cooking. Mix powdered or concentrated maple syrup with water as needed. Combine two tablespoons of water with a tablespoon of powdered egg for the equivalent of one fresh egg. Add water to transform concentrated soups, dried fruit, dehydrated juices, hot chocolate mixes, and puddings into delicious eating.

Even meats and vegetables may be enjoyed by campers through the new freeze-dry process, which requires no refrigeration. Freeze-dried beef, chicken, and meatballs, as well as fruits, vegetables, stews, and salads provide a varied menu to satisfy many

102

individual tastes on a canoe-camping trip.

A necessary staple is bread. For camping, coarse breads, like rye, whole wheat, and pumpernickel, are recommended because they are more filling and last longer than white bread. Other breadstuffs that keep well are hardtack, rye krisp, and heavy crackers. Should your bread ration run out, baking outdoors is quite simple with the many commercial mixes. Bread, cookies, muffins, corn bread, and other products already packed in waterproof envelopes are stocked in most supermarts, and they are easy to prepare in the wilderness.

One-pot meals are very popular on camping trips. Such easy-to-make foods as slumgullion, Irish stew, and chili provide nourishing one-course meals.

Other nourishing, quick-energy foods include syrup, jam, honey, sugar, candy, and malted milk tablets. These should be taken in sumptuous quantities. On long canoe trips, teen-agers often like to keep a canvas bag filled with hard candy tied to a thwart, where they can easily reach it when hunger strikes.

A quick-energy emergency ration that you can prepare at home provides much bulk and nutrition. To make this food, melt a bar of sweet chocolate and stir in a handful of cold cereal flakes, some raisins and/or dates or shredded coconut, and a half cup of chopped nuts. Mix the ingredients well, remove from the stove, and pour into a shallow buttered pan. After the mixture cools, cut it into squares, wrap in waxed paper, and seal. This all-inclusive energy food will keep you from getting hungry on a long, demanding trip.

When planning the food necessary for your canoe trip, plan three meals and a snack a day for each member of the party for every day afloat. Then add, for good measure, one extra day's food for each person; campers eat more on a trip than at home.

Check camping handbooks for suggested grub lists. However, keep in mind that most grub lists are geared to men and that they should not be followed strictly. The only grub lists that are important to your party are those that suit the personal needs of the individuals. Take into account your group's wide variation in likes, dislikes, and allergies when you plan their daily food needs.

When you have a menu planned for each meal every day, figure the quantities of each food needed for the entire trip. After purchasing the necessary supplies, prepare them for transporting. Take the foods out of their original bulky, fragile boxes. Pack loose food, such as powdered milk and sugar, in plastic waterproof bags; include the clipped instructions, and tie the bags at the top. Attach a shipping tag to the bag, with the contents and quantity marked in waterproof India ink. For items that melt or come in glass containers, like butter, honey, jam, and peanut butter, transfer the contents to tins with press-on or screw-type lids. Then stow all bags and tins into packsacks.

LOADING FOR THE TRIP   After all supplies and equipment have been gathered, stored in packsacks, and transported to the launching site for your canoe trip, it is time to consider loading procedures.

First, lay the heaviest items, such as tent, food, and hardware, in the bottom of the canoe on a low bed of evergreen boughs or a packboard. Pile the lighter equipment, such as clothing and bedding, in packs on top. Lash together your extra paddle, fishing rods, and axe, and securely wedge them beside the duffel in the bottom. In that way, they won't fall overboard should the canoe lurch. Cover all duffel amidship with a tarpaulin, and lash the corners of the tarp to the thwarts.

As mentioned earlier, a loaded craft should have a freeboard of at least seven inches in smooth water and more in rough water. To obtain this safety margin, you may have to rearrange your cargo a few times. Experience will help you to judge the proper weight distribution of cargo and passengers.

A TWO-CANOE PARTY   When two canoes are used on a canoe-camping trip, food, sleeping gear, cooking utensils, and shelter should be divided between the two as equally as possible. Each canoe should be a self-contained unit, carrying all the equipment needed by its crew.

The canoes should use the buddy system and stay together. The most experienced canoeist rides in the lead canoe. The second canoe follows at a close but safe distance, for it is advisable to keep the canoes in constant communication regarding map course, sights along the way, hazards, weather developments, portage paths, and possible campsites.

PORTAGING   Carrying your canoe and duffel around rapids or waterfalls or across land joining two lakes is hard work. But portaging gives a change of pace to lake or river cruising, and the expectation of different scenery adds to the interest of portages.

In well-traveled canoe waters, portage trails are usually marked. When you have to make a portage, unload your canoe and place the duffel on high ground. Transport the canoe first. Use adequate help in carrying the canoe; the two- and four-man carries discussed earlier are the most efficient.

Such unwieldy articles as fishing rods, paddles, and axe, tied into a single bundle, facilitate carrying across portage paths. They may be toted as a loose bundle or lashed to the thwarts of the canoe.

Concentrate all duffel into packs, so that there are no unnecessary trips. Break up long portages by carrying duffel in relays of a quarter-mile or so. Set down one load and return for another, bringing it forward in a second stage. In this way, you combine the labor over the trail with a return recuperative hike, which is less fatiguing.

SETTING UP CAMP   Once you have arrived at a campsite, unload your canoe, carry it safely from the water, and turn it upside down for storage. Decide on your tent and kitchen locations, and your latrine and garbage spots. Set up camp before you go swimming, fishing, visiting, or exploring.

All members of the party are needed to set up camp. Clear the tent site of rocks, sticks, and debris. Pitch your tent on a windswept elevated clearing, away from tall trees if possible, to insure proper drainage, mosquito protection, privacy, and a view. Face the tent north or northeast in a spot that will receive the morning sun to burn off the dewy moisture and to awaken you. After you pitch the tent, dig drainage ditches around it.

Your kitchen area should include space for a cooking fire, for stacking firewood, and for all kitchen equipment. Place your equipment in position. Keep your wood supply covered with a tarp or large slabs of bark at night and during threatening weather.

Always dig a garbage pit and bury your garbage, covering it with soil. Burn out, flatten, and bury tin cans. Never leave food exposed. A dirty camp attracts flies and other pesky insects. Besides, it spoils the beauty of the wilderness and leaves behind an unsightly mess for other campers.

Most well-traveled canoe trails have latrines, but should you need to make your own, the straddle trench, or pit, is easy to dig. Place it downhill some distance from your camp and water supply. Choose a secluded place to insure privacy, which can be increased with the addition of a screen of underbrush or with a canvas or tarp wall.

Dig the latrine trench two to three feet deep. Pile the dirt along the sides, where it can be kicked back into the trench each time the latrine is used. Use two parallel logs raised about 18 inches above the ground for a comfortable seat over the pit. If an outdoor latrine is to be used for several days, purify it periodically with wood ashes or chloride of lime, which can be purchased at a lumberyard. Buy five pounds of lime and pack it in a waterproof bag if you plan to camp in one place for a week or more.

After you have set up camp, explore your new-found neighborhood. Wearing heavy shoes, hike inland with a companion and make a half-circle around your camp. Of course, take along your compass and your emergency whistle. If you are on an island, explore its boundaries. Look for alternate canoe-docking areas to use if a wind comes up to prevent you from using the docking site near your camp.

COMMON SENSE PRECAUTIONS   Always be careful with campfires. Start the fire in a safe clear place, away from trees, brush, and equipment and sheltered from winds. When the area is cleared to bare earth, place dry, light tinder and kindling on the bottom, medium-sized wood chunks and larger logs on top. The cooking fire is built between two logs placed side by side. The logs are a little farther apart on the front end than at the back. Place the frying pan on the wide end and the smaller pots on the narrow end. For the evening campfire, the wood may be arranged in a square log-cabin pattern or a pyramid shape. To put out the fire, douse it first with water and then shovel dirt over the entire area. After the fire is completely extinguished, pour on another bucket of water.

Follow a schedule for getting up, preparing and eating meals, working, playing, and going to bed. You will have a better camp and a better time if you police your campsite regularly, organize your personal duffel, maintain an adequate supply of drinking water and firewood, dispose of garbage, and keep yourself clean and neat.

Slow down and move in a tempo that fits your outdoor life. Enjoy the scenery and the leisure time. If you play too hard in the hot sun and begin to feel

COOKING FIRE SET

CAMPFIRE SET

faint or dizzy, stop at once, seek shade, and slow down. Heat exhaustion is more serious than sunstroke.

Visit other campers and exchange stories with them. Canoe-campers are generally congenial people, and most enjoy company. From them, you may learn more about good fishing spots, campsites, portage trails, and other interesting information.

Try keeping a diary so that when questions arise over directions, portages, campsites, or landmarks, you have an accurate record. Throughout your trip, jot down comments on paddling time, general and personal equipment evaluation, the grub list, campsites, and other information that will improve your next trip.

When you break camp, leave the site neater than you found it. Remove as many evidences of your stay as possible, leaving the area in its natural beauty. Before pushing off, look around the area for equipment that may have been overlooked. An unwritten law of the woods obligates each camper to leave at a campsite as much, or more, firewood as he found. The next party may arrive at the site late at night, during a rainstorm, or too fatigued to search for wood.

Cooperate on all chores cheerfully, both in the canoe and in camp. You will find that paddling through beautiful scenery, fishing in well-stocked waters, and camping in the outdoors will bring together a group as no other cooperative activity can.

CHAPTER SEVEN

WATER ROUTES AND MAP SOURCES

Opportunities for canoeing exist in all parts of the United States. You need not wander far to enjoy the sport. You can paddle your craft quietly and safely on a nearby stream, lake, or river, or you may explore a canoeing territory far from home. If you do not know where to go or if you desire to explore new places, you can obtain canoeing information from a wide variety of sources. Many of these sources also offer literature on camping, paddle techniques, safety, and other useful canoeing facts.

The following national organizations include canoeing in their programs: The American Red Cross, Boy Scouts, Girl Scouts, Explorer Scouts, Prairie Club, Sierra Club, and the American Youth Hostel. Refer to the yellow pages of your telephone directory for the chapter nearest you and for listings of local hiking, camping, and outdoor clubs.

Much canoeing information is distributed through the magazine and regional divisions of the American Canoe Association. Their national office

Canoe waterways lead to many scenic areas. In the Algoma district of Northern Ontario, the narrow Carp River winds between rocky cliffs to join Lake Superior near the Trans-Canada Highway.

is at 400 Eastern Avenue, New Haven, Connecticut 06513.

Pamphlets, books, and magazines will be sent to you in response to a letter to the Tourism Division, the Department of Conservation, or the Chamber of Commerce of any state capital. Materials from some of these sources, and others, are named in the following lists, arranged according to regions of the United States.

EASTERN STATES

Adirondack Canoe Routes, Recreation Circular 7, Conservation Department, Albany, New York 12200.

Big Load Afloat, Inland Waterways, The American Waterways Operators, Inc., 1250 Connecticut Avenue, Suite 502, Washington, D. C. 20036.

Canoeable Waterways of New York, Pageant Press, Inc., 130 West 42nd Street, New York, New York 10036.

Canoe Guide to Western Pennsylvania, American Youth Hostels, 6300 Fifth Avenue, Pittsburgh, Pennsylvania 15232.

Canoeing White Water in North Virginia and Northeast West Virginia, Louis Mascia, 3430 Lee Highway, Fairfax, Virginia 22030.

Canoe Trips in Florida, American Camping Association, Florida Section, E. M. Schmidt, Bradford Woods, Martinsville, Indiana 46151.

Exploring the Little Rivers of New Jersey, Rutgers University Press, New Brunswick, New Jersey 08900.

The Historical and Famous Delaware River, Delaware River Basin Commission, Box 360, Trenton, New Jersey 08603.

Maine Canoeing, Department of Economic Development, State House, Augusta, Maine 04330.

New England Canoeing Guide, The Appalachian Mountain Club, 5 Joy Street, Boston, Massachusetts 02108.

Tennessee Division of State Parks, 203 Cordell Hull Building, Nashville, Tennessee 37219.

Unexplored Okefenokee Swamp, Georgia Department of Industry and Trade, 100 State Capitol, Atlanta, Georgia 30334.

MIDWESTERN STATES

Canoe Trails of Michigan, Michigan Tourist Council, Lansing, Michigan 48900.

Crane Lake Commercial Club, Crane Lake, Minnesota 55725 (Superior-Quetico area).

Ely Commercial Club, Ely, Minnesota 55731 (Superior-Quetico area).

Gunflint Trail Association, Grand Marais, Minnesota 55604 (Superior-Quetico area).

The Historic Fox Valley Canoe Trail, The Chicagoland Canoe Base, Ralph C. Frese, 4019 North Narragansett, Chicago, Illinois 60634.

Illinois Canoeing Guide, Illinois Department of Conservation, Springfield, Illinois 62600.

Indiana Canoe Trails, Indiana Department of Conservation, Division of Water Resources, Room 609, State Office Building, Indianapolis, Indiana 46204.

Iowa Canoe Trips, Iowa Conservation Commission, East 7th and Court Avenues, Des Moines, Iowa 50300.

Lincoln Heritage Canoe Trail (Sangamon River), Jack Johnson, 12 North Cottonhill, Springfield, Illinois 62700.

Little-Known Minnesota Rivers Great for Canoeing and **Wilderness Canoe Trips,** Visitor Information Center, Department of Economic Development, 57 West 7th Street, St. Paul, Minnesota 55102.

Missouri Ozark Waterways, Missouri Conservation Commission, Jefferson City, Missouri 65101.

Ohio Canoe Trails, Ohio Department of Natural Resources, Division of Watercraft, 802 Ohio Departments Building, Columbus, Ohio 43215.

River Maps of the Current and Jacks Fork, S. G. Adams Printing and Stationery Company, 10th and Olive Streets, St. Louis, Missouri 63101.

Superior-Quetico Atlas, W. A. Fisher Company, Virginia, Minnesota 55792.

Where To Fish in Kansas, Forestry Commission, Box 1028, Pratt, Kansas 67124.

Wisconsin Water Trails, Wisconsin Conservation Department, Madison, Wisconsin 53500.

WESTERN STATES

Arizona State Parks Board, Room 431, State Capitol Building, Phoenix, Arizona 85007.

California State Park System, Department of Parks and Recreation, P. O. Box 2390, Sacramento, California 95811.

Colorado Department of Game, Fish and Parks, 6060 Broadway, Denver, Colorado 80216.

Idaho Department of Commerce and Development, Room 108, State House, Boise, Idaho 83702.

Oregon Travel Information Division, Room A, State Highway Department, Salem, Oregon 97301.

Texas Parks and Wildlife Department, John H. Reagan Building, Austin, Texas 78701.

Utah State Parks and Recreation Commission, 132 South Second West, Salt Lake City, Utah 84101.

Washington Tourist Promotion Division, General Administration Building, Olympia, Washington 98501.

Wyoming Recreation Commission, State Office Building, Cheyenne, Wyoming 82001.

CANOEING IN CANADA Canada offers especially exciting canoeing opportunities. Two excellent areas in the upper Midwest and Canada are the Superior-Quetico area and Algonquin Provincial Park. The Superior-Quetico canoe country in Minnesota and Ontario, Canada, has retained in its woods and waters the primeval character of colonial America. It comprises an area of 14,000 square miles, most of it ideal for canoe travel. Algonquin Provincial Park, in Ontario, Canada, less than 300 miles from the United States-Canada border, is similar to Superior-Quetico. This vast but safe wilderness of 3,000 square miles of sparkling water and virgin forests is set aside for canoe-camping. Over 5,000 people, 80 percent of them from the United States, camp in this area each season.

116

Information on canoeing in Canada may be obtained from the following sources.

British Columbia Government Travel Bureau, Victoria, British Columbia.

Canadian Government Travel Bureau, 150 Kent Street, Ottawa, Ontario. (Bureau will supply address of the Travel Bureau of each province as well as furnish literature on canoeing throughout Canada. United States offices include: 680 Fifth Avenue, New York City, New York 10019; 155 Jackson Street, San Francisco, California 94111; and 14 other cities.)

Canadian National Railways, Montreal.

Manitoba Bureau of Travel and Publicity, Winnipeg, Manitoba.

Northern Stores Department, Hudson's Bay Company, Hudson's Bay House, Winnipeg. (Booklet *U-Paddle Canoes* explains how you can rent a canoe from one post, take your cruise, and finish at a distant post without backtracking.)

Nova Scotia Tourist and Information Bureau, Halifax, Nova Scotia.

Ontario Department of Travel and Publicity, Toronto, Ontario.

Province of Quebec Tourist Bureau, Quebec City, Quebec.

CHAPTER EIGHT

HISTORY OF CANOEING

Primitive canoes were hollowed out of logs, fashioned from animal skins, or woven with reeds. Such crude crafts probably were used by people as far back in time as the Stone Age. Therefore, the birchbark canoe of the American Eastern Woodland Indian was the product of perhaps thousands of years of experimentation with water craft. When the colonists arrived on the eastern shore of the United States, they found the Indians' mode of travel ideal for moving inland to explore and settle. So perfect was the birchbark canoe that the canoes of today have essentially the same design.

Although many pioneers marched westward on foot, rode horseback, and traveled in covered wagons and ox carts, the Canadian Voyageurs met the challenge of the northland's large lakes and numerous rivers with the Indian canoe. The Voyageurs were English, Scotch, and French men who settled in the picturesque hamlets along the St. Lawrence River.

*The Voyageurs pulled their canoes ashore and turned them up on an angle
for night shelter.*

The Voyageurs were an ambitious and colorful
group. Their unofficial uniform was a red woolen
cap, brightly colored sash, beaded ditty bag, and
Indian style clothes. The craft of the Voyageurs was
a huge yellow birchbark canoe thirty feet long, with
flaring sides, pointed ends, and a high prow, propelled by red paddles. In their fifteen-hour paddling day, the twelve crewmen on each canoe transported three tons of cargo on the Great Lakes and
other wilderness waterways. Heavy stores of such
manufactured goods as axes, traps, guns, blankets,
and clothing were in great demand by the Indians.

These sturdy canoes, paddled by Voyageurs, could carry nine people and their duffel as well as a heavy cargo of trading goods.

Exploratory trips along uncharted water trails by the Voyageurs and other adventurers contributed to the development of two nations. These hardy traders and explorers penetrated the northern part of the United States and Canada, and by the mid-1600's, they had traveled deep into the interior of the continent. This movement was led by several noted men, including Jacques Cartier, who bartered with the Micmac Indians for beaver, thus beginning the fur trade, and Père Marquette, a Jesuit missionary who explored the Illinois territory along the Mississippi River.

Throughout the ages, sea-faring people have held ceremonies to test the hardiness of new ship-mates and to appease their gods for a swift journey. The Voyageurs were no different. They initiated their new crewmen by dipping cedar boughs into the water and sprinkling those making their first trip into the hinterland. A salvo of shots closed the ceremony that entitled the crewmen, forever after, to wear feather plumes in their caps. Today's canoe clubs often follow this tradition, initiating new members in Indian or explorer attire and holding ceremonies and competitions to test the members' skills.

Sports and pleasure canoeing was popularized in the last half of the 19th century with the development of the Rob Roy and Peterborough canoes. The Rob Roy, built in 1865 by Scotish canoeist John Macgregor, was a kayak-style craft for one man with a double-bladed paddle. Developed about 1900, the Peterborough canoe was a cedar-strip canoe fashioned like the Indian birchbark and propelled by a single-bladed paddle. With modifications, the Rob Roy became a sailing-racing craft. The Peterborough canoe was the forerunner of the modern sport and cruising canoe.

Cruising and camping enthusiasts still have the opportunity to enjoy the waterways of the early traders, hunters, explorers, and Indians. As the sport gains in popularity, more areas are set aside for canoeing, new canoe clubs are established, and better canoeing equipment is developed. In addition, a widening range of activities is available to the skilled canoeist.

Attachable equipment has made the canoe a most versatile craft. By adding a motor, the canoeist can travel quickly through rough water and can shorten the time spent in backtracking a familiar route. Canoe sailing has become a sport apart from traditional canoeing. Each year national and international canoe sailing organizations meet for strenuous sailing competition.

White-water canoeing, or paddling through turbulent waters, was once highly competitive among a few canoeists, but it is now becoming a family sport. Organized groups, like the Canoe Cruisers of Northern Vermont and the Hoofers Club of Wisconsin, schedule family teams for white-water trips. In white-water meets, beginners canoe in tamer rivers, where quiet stretches are mixed with lively runs.

Throughout the country, canoe regattas, or races, marathons, and historical celebrations are staged annually by local business groups, canoe clubs, camps, and sports associations. These community programs include races, exhibitions, demonstrations, floating trips, and picnics.

Local victories in some of these events can lead a highly skilled canoeist into national and international competition. Being selected for Olympic competition is perhaps the greatest honor for a canoeist. Nineteen nations competed in the first Olympic ca-

White-water canoeing is a fast-moving sport requiring skill and control.

noeing competition at Berlin, Germany, in 1936. Since then, more canoeing events have been added, including white-water kayaking, straight racing, and slalom racing; and more nations have entered competition. In the 1964 Olympics, 50 teams competed.

Tryouts for the United States canoeing team are held in all regions of the country. After the team of twelve men and four women is selected, the group

In large birchbark canoes, six-man teams representing all the provinces of Canada begin the Voyageur Race as part of Expo '67. The 3,283-mile trip lasted 104 days and ended in Montreal, Canada.

Midway in Expo '67's Voyageur Race, the British Columbia team demonstrates the fine precision paddling that marks the expert canoeist.

assembles for vigorous training under the scrutiny of the Olympic coach. Then, every four years, the world's best canoeists represent their countries in the most colorful of all canoeing spectacles.

ABOUT THE AUTHOR

John Malo is an avid sportsman. He spends his summer, winter, and spring vacations and many weekends canoeing, camping, fishing, and hiking. He was one of the first scuba divers to explore the underwater coral formations off Key Largo, Florida, in an area which became the Pennekamp State Park, the first underwater park in existence. In 1953 Mr. Malo coached the city championship baseball team of Foreman High School in Chicago, Illinois. That same year he was named Coach of the Year by Chicagoland Prep Writers.

While a student at Northwestern University, Evanston, Illinois, he was a camp counselor during his summer vacations. One of his campers was Adlai Stevenson III, who recalls, "In my boyhood days when attending a summer camp in Wisconsin, it was my good fortune to have as a counselor John Malo, who initiated me into the exciting and enriching realism of woods and waters. He taught me the art of canoeing and took me on my first overnight canoe trip."

After college graduation, Mr. Malo spent a year of graduate study in Europe, taking time off from studies for hiking, kayaking, mountain climbing, and skiing.

He is now assistant principal of Foreman High School. Over the years Mr. Malo has taught canoeing skills to many of his students, and they have shared his exciting adventures on uncharted waters in the United States and Canada. In addition, as sponsor of the local Izaak Walton Club, he teaches other young people how to explore and appreciate woodlands and canoe waterways.

127

John Malo and two Izaak Walton Club members hike to their canoe for a fishing trip.